La Traviata

BLACK DOG OPERA LIBRARY

La Traviata

GIUSEPPI VERDI

TEXT BY DANIEL S. BRINK

BLACK DOG
& LEVENTHAL
PUBLISHERS
NEW YORK

The enclosed compact discs ℗ 1988 EMI Records Ltd.
Product of EMI-Capitol Music Special Markets, 1750 North Vine Street,
Los Angeles, California 90028.

Published by
Black Dog & Leventhal Publishers, Inc.
151 West 19th Street
New York, NY 10011

Distributed by
Workman Publishing Company
708 Broadway
New York, NY 10003

Designed by Alleycat Design, Inc.

Series editor: Jessica MacMurray

Photo Research: Diana Gongora

Book manufactured in Singapore

ISBN: 1-57912-017-2

h g f e d c b

FOREWORD

*L*a Traviata—one of the greatest works from the most celebrated opera composers in history—is one of the mainstays of the operatic stage. Verdi achieved a magical and delicate balance between a tragic love story, a socially and politically courageous plot and some of the most powerful and heart-breaking music ever written.

You will hear the entire opera on the two compact discs included on the inside front and back covers of this book. As you explore the book, you will discover the story behind the opera and its creation, the life of the composer, biographies of the principal singers and conductor, and the opera's text, or libretto, both in Italian and English. Expert commentary has been added to the libretto to aid in your appreciation and to highlight key moments in the score.

Enjoy this book and enjoy the music.

ABOUT THE AUTHOR

*D*aniel S. Brink is the Artistic Advisor and Principal Coach/Accompanist for the Colorado Opera Festival, Artistic Director for the Company Singers, a development program for young operatic hopefuls and Artistic Director/Conductor of the Colorado Springs Choral Society small ensemble, MOSIAC. Mr. Brink is a lecturer in Music and principal accompanist at The Colorado College, and has performed extensively in the United States and Europe. He is a highly regarded director, recitalist, teacher, adjudicator and writer.

ACKNOWLEDGEMENTS

I would like to thank Annette Megneys of the Colorado College Music Library and Jan Boothroyd, Executive Director of the Colorado Opera Festival for their invaluable assistance in researching this project. I would also like to thank my editor, Jessica MacMurray, whose influence afforded me the opportunity to write about these beloved works.

GIUSEPPE VERDI
(1813-1901)

La Traviata

Giuseppe Verdi—the name has been synonymous with opera for a century and a half. He was born into an Italy divided under French and Austrian rule, and his work would eventually play a part in Italy's unification. His voice gave Italy a musical identity when the whole artistic world was proclaiming Richard Wagner the wave of the future. Over a sixty-year career, he gave the world 32 operas, including rewrites, which were extensive. He wrote countless other works, the most famous of which is his *Requiem,* written on the death of Alesandro Manzoni, an Italian author whose work had inspired Verdi in his youth.

He was born on October 10, 1813, in the small village of Le Roncole in northern Italy. His father, Carlo Verdi, a poor peasant, ran the local combination shop (an inn and tavern) and farmed a small plot of land. Verdi had only one sibling, a younger sister who was retarded and who died in her teenage years. As a child, he showed an early interest in music. It is said that he used to follow an itinerant fiddle player all around the village, and that he would be transfixed by the organ music at church on Sundays, sometimes forgetting his

ADELINA PATTI AS VIOLETTA,
CIRCA 1890

duties as acolyte. And sometime before his eighth birthday, Verdi's father gave him an old spinet—a small harpsichord—whose popularity had already long since been supplanted by the piano.

Carlo Verdi had dealings with Antonio Barezzi, a leading businessman in the larger town of Busseto three miles away. Barezzi owned the city's department store and was the president of the local Philharmonic Society, an amateur group which performed at local events and played concerts throughout the region. When Giuseppe was ten years old, his father and Barezzi arranged for him to go and board with a cobbler in Busseto, so that his general education could be taken over by Don Pietro Seletti, a priest at the local cathedral, and his musical education could be formalized under Ferdinando Provesi, music director at the cathedral.

The young Verdi proved himself a diligent worker, though he was more successful in his musical studies than in his other subjects. And every Sunday he walked the three miles to Le Roncole to play the organ at the village church. As Verdi's skills advanced, he composed marches and overtures for the Philharmonic Society and occasionally served as its conductor. At age 16, he moved into Barezzi's home and helped him both conduct his business affairs and coordinate his musical leadership in the city.

In 1832, it was decided that Giuseppe's talent warranted sending him to the Milan Conservatory. Milan was the musical capital of Italy and the home of La Scala, Italy's leading opera house. At age 19, with the financial backing of Barezzi and a local charitable foundation, Verdi moved to Milan. However, he was not accepted at the Conservatory, and the reasons why were never given. He was sent instead to study privately with Vincenzo Lavigna, a respected conductor at La Scala, under whose tutelage Verdi thrived. Years later, when a desire was expressed to change the name of the Milan conservatory to the Verdi Conservatory, Verdi refused to grant permission, saying, "They didn't want me when I was young, they can't have me now that I'm old."

ACT II, HER MAJESTY'S THEATRE, LONDON, 1856

In the summer of 1833, Verdi's former mentor, Provesi, died, leaving the music director's post in Busseto open. Barezzi and the Philharmonic Society wanted Verdi for the job, while the leadership at the cathedral backed another candidate. This conflict divided the town into two camps and eventually required government intervention. In the end, Verdi won the position. The dispute had lasted three years, by which time Verdi's studies with Lavigna were completed. And his time in Milan had exposed him to the triumphs of the leading opera composers of the era—the sparkling comedies of Rossini, the masterful melodic gift of Bellini, and the seductive charm of Donizetti. He had also been presented with a libretto, *Oberto, Conte di San Bonifacio,* and had already begun work on before he returned to Busseto to being his new job.

With his education complete and a paying position in Busseto, he married Barezzi's eldest daughter, Margherita, with whom he had fallen in love over the years of his close association with her father. He settled into his new job and family life, but continued to work on his opera and court the appropriate connections in Milan to see it produced. Verdi was introduced to Bartolomeo Merelli, the new impresario at La Scala, and after a long period of alternating promise and disappointment, he was granted a production of *Oberto* in the fall of 1839. The opera was a huge success and prompted Merelli to commission three more operas from Verdi. His new professional course appeared to be set, so Verdi resigned his position in Busseto and moved to Milan.

While success was the order of the day in his work, Verdi's personal life was unraveling tragically. Since their marriage, Margherita had borne Verdi two children, a daughter, Virginia, born in March of 1837, and a son, Icilio, born in July of 1838. One month and a day after Icilio's birth, Virginia suddenly died of an unidentified illness. Fourteen months later, in October of 1839, Icilio died.

Again, the cause was unknown. The young parents were horrified. Then, on June 18, 1840, Margherita died of encephalitis. Alone and devastated, Verdi pressed on through the premiere of his second opera, *Un Giorno di Regno,* the only comedy he would attempt until his final opera, *Falstaff,* debuted in 1893. *Un Giorno* was a dismal failure.

Professionally and personally defeated, Verdi wanted to stop composing and canceled his contract with Merelli, becoming a near recluse. Several months later, Verdi ran into Merelli on the street, and the impresario encouraged him to resume his work. Gradually, Verdi responded, and his next effort, *Nabucco,* a biblical epic on the Babylonian captivity of the Jews, was the overwhelmingly successful result. A particu-

GIUSEPPE VERDI

lar chorus from the opera, *Va, pensiero, sull'ali dorate* (Fly, thought, on golden wings), is sung by the captive Hebrews as they recall the beauty of their homeland and long for freedom. The Milanese public, under oppressive Austrian rule, identified with the chorus's sentiment, and from the first performance it became the anthem for an Italian nation longing for independence. Many years later, at Verdi's funeral, the thousands who lined the streets began singing this chorus spontaneously as his body was carried by.

With the success of *Nabucco,* Verdi's financial worries were over. Between 1843 and 1850, he produced 13 new operas, most of which were warmly accepted by the public and critics alike. While not all of these remain in the popular repertoire today, they represent a steady growth in Verdi's musical style and dramatic ideals. The construction of these operas owes much to Verdi's predecessors. They are made up of a series of "set numbers"—arias which reveal the inner thoughts of the characters and recitatives and ensembles that advance the dramatic action. Like Rossini, Bellini and Donizetti, the kings of the bel canto era, Verdi's primary musical tool was a gift for melody, where the orchestra plays a secondary role to the voice. (In contrast, in Wagner's music dramas, the orchestra almost becomes another character, and its contribution is essential to the dramatic flow.)

Of these early Verdi works, *Ernani, Macbeth* and perhaps *Luisa Miller* are the most frequently performed today, although all of them have received periodic revivals and even complete recordings in the past few decades. These three, however, best represent Verdi's capacity for emotional intensity and the vital, earthy quality that distinguishes his best work. Most of the operas of this period take place against the backdrop of political intrigue, and during these years Verdi had many run-ins with the Austrian censors. In the minds of the Italian people, Verdi was

increasingly becoming a political figure, and lines from his operas became bywords for the resistance to Austrian occupation. In his opera, Attila, for example, we hear the line *"Avrai tu L'universo, resti l'Italia a me"* (You may have the rest of the world, leave Italy to me). This became the motto of the *Risorgamento,* the movement to unite Italy under one native ruler. In his *La Battaglia di Legnano,* there is a scene in which an imprisoned officer of the resistance throws himself into the river below, distraught at his inability to join his fellows in the march on the oppressor. At a performance of this opera in 1849, a soldier in the audience was so caught up in the passion of the moment that he threw himself out of the gallery and into the orchestra pit. Miraculously, no one was hurt.

Also during this period, to the annoyance of the Austrian police, the walls of most major cities in Italy were covered with graffiti saying *"Viva Verdi."* This cry of the underground had a double meaning: First, it was for many an acknowledgment of Giuseppe Verdi as a voice for the unification movement; it was also an acrostic for *"Viva Vittorio Emmanuele, Re D'Italia"* (Long live Victor Emmanuel, King of Italy). Vittorio Emmanuele was then king of Piedmont, the northwestern region of the peninsula, and he was thought to be a sympathetic ruler. He would eventually become king of a mostly united Italy, and reign from 1861 to 1878. For himself, Verdi remained an unwilling political hero, saying throughout his life that he knew nothing of politics. He was even pressed into service for a time as a representative from Busseto and its district to the first Italian Parliament, but thought of himself as an ill-informed and ineffectual legislator.

The intervening years also saw important developments in Verdi's personal life. Giuseppina Strepponi was a leading soprano of the time, and she had known and worked with Verdi since the beginnings of his career. Her influence was instrumental in ensuring that his first opera, *Oberto,* was staged, and she had created the leading role of Abigaille in his triumphant *Nabucco.* They had remained good friends, but sometime during the middle of the 1840s, friendship blossomed into love. She had retired from the stage and was teaching in Paris, where their affair probably began. By the end of the decade, she was living with Verdi in Busseto, much to the consternation of his father-in-law and mentor, Antonio Barrezzi, his parents, and the rest of the populace of his hometown, who shunned them both. Their relationship was idyllic, however, and after an inexplicable wait of over ten years, they were married in 1859. She remained his indispensable lover, helpmate and confidante for the rest of their lives. She died in 1899, a year and a half before Verdi's death.

In 1848, Verdi purchased his sprawling estate at Sant'Agata. This was to be his home and haven for the rest of his life. Over the years, he had become a shrewd businessman, carefully overseeing the contracts for performances of all

his works. Now he applied those same skills to the occupation of his ancestors, running a large and very successful farm in what was, at first glance, a flat and forbidding landscape. He studied modern farming techniques to improve the yield of the soil, and he contributed much to the area's depressed economy by employing many of the local peasants with whom he dealt generously. Through the years, farming proved to be an even greater passion for Verdi than music, and it contributed greatly to his wealth. He always thought of himself as a simple man from the country, and it was in this environment that his creative energies were most acute.

The years from 1850 to 1853 saw the creation of three of Verdi's most enduring works, *Rigoletto, Il Trovatore* and *La Traviata.* Until these operas, the characters to whom Verdi was attracted were mainly historical and monochromatic. A character was either all good or all

ACT III, METROPOLITAN OPERA, 1981

bad, and Verdi's capacity to represent that in musical terms had developed well. Now, however, he actively sought enigmatic characters, ones who were both hostile and loving, hero and outcast. As a result, the way in which Verdi structured his operas underwent a change. Where his basic unit of construction had always been the aria, now it became the scene, and the result was heightened dramatic effect.

Rigoletto was based on Victor Hugo's *Le Roi S'Amuse (The King Amuses Himself)*. During its preparation, Verdi had no end of troubles with the censors, who initially banned the libretto altogether. They no doubt thought the corrupt king in the story could all too easily be equated in the public mind with any number of the current Italian leaders placed in power by Austria. Through lengthy negotiation, Verdi was able to gain approval for the libretto, after changing the characters' names and the time and locale of the action, But he then had only 40 days to complete the score prior to its scheduled premiere.

Rigoletto is the story of a deformed jester whose beloved daughter is seduced by the libertine duke in whose court the jester entertains. Seeking revenge, he hires an assassin to kill the duke. Instead, the jester's daughter is accidentally killed as she attempts to save the duke who has loved her and left her. This work was an exceptionally lurid tale for the Italian stage at that time. Rigoletto, the hunchback jester, is both a loving father and an attempted murderer. Gilda, his daughter (who was raped), sacrifices her life for her rapist, and the decadent duke gets off scot-free. There are no unqualified heroes or completely innocent victims here, and it was a challenge to the moral sensibilities of the day. Still, the public was enthralled, though the critics dutifully objected to the subject matter.

Verdi's next endeavor was to set *El Trovador,* a Spanish drama by Gutierrez. It is a dark and complex story centered on the gypsy, Azucena. She is driven both by her vendetta against the Count di Luna and by her all-consuming love for her son, Manrico. This dual nature and moral ambiguity, as in the character of Rigoletto, was attractive to Verdi. He was very keen on maintaining the intensity of the Spanish version and rejected the work of his librettists several times during the creative process. What resulted was a taut little drama with a wealth of deeply passionate music, though much of the real action of the story takes place offstage. The opera, *Il Trovatore,* opened in Rome on January 19, 1853, and was an unqualified success. It immediately began to be produced all over the operatic world.

In the winter of 1851-52, while he was working on *Il Trovatore* for its Roman debut, Verdi and Strepponi went to Paris. There, he saw LA DAME AUX CAMELIAS, a new play by Alexandre Dumas fils, based on the author's 1848 novel, *Camille.* Verdi may have been familiar with the widely read novel, as well as with the play, which was the rage in Paris. It was the character of Camille —called Violetta in the opera—that piqued Verdi's interest. Like the hunchback, Rigoletto, and the Gypsy, Azucena, the courtesan Violetta was a figure that would be shunned by polite society. Yet she is ennobled by her capacity for loving self-sacrifice. Verdi immediately commissioned a libretto from Francesco Maria Piave, who had contributed the verses for six of his previous operas including the highly esteemed *Macbeth* and *Rigoletto.* The opera, *La Traviata,* would be produced on March 6, 1853, at the Teatro La Fenice in Venice, only seven weeks after the world was first introduced to *Il Trovatore* in Rome.

Verdi spent the bulk of 1852 working on *Il Trovatore* and *La Traviata* concurrently. After his stay in Rome for the preparation and premiere of *Il Trovatore,* he returned to Busseto. There he received disturbing news from a friend in Venice. Fanny Salvini-Donatelli, the soprano who he had hired to create the role of Violetta, had been giving some substandard performances, and Verdi was warned that her work might mar the premiere of *La Traviata.* Writing quickly to Venice, Verdi requested the role be recast, but the soprano he preferred was unavailable, and it was contractually too late to search for another.

Verdi arrived in Venice only 13 days prior to the premiere. It had been his custom to arrive several weeks before an opening and meticulously oversee every facet of rehearsal and production. He also usually spent these final weeks orchestrating the new work, never promising the orchestral parts in the contract until the day before the final rehearsal. It is possible, in this case, that these last 13 days were actually spent feverishly orchestrating the score, and Verdi had no time to attend rehearsals. There is no correspondence from the time that recorded how he spent his time or what his reactions were to the preparation of his new work.

The premiere was a complete fiasco. The audience, polite at first, was increasingly cool as the opera progressed, and during the final act, in which Violetta is dying of consumption, there was continuous laughter. It seems that Salvini-Donatelli was not only the picture of health but rather plump, and her persistent cough became a source of comic relief rather than pathos. The critics acknowledged that the singers were most of the problem. The tenor singing the role of Violetta's lover, Alfredo, was losing his voice, and the baritone, in the role of Alfredo's father, Germont, put nothing into his performance. He had been the creator of the plum role of *Rigoletto* and was a well-known interpreter of the

ACT II, SCENE II,
GUESTS
MASQUERADING
AT FLORA'S
PARTY. GLYNDE-
BOURNE FESTIVAL
OPERA

title role in Verdi's *Macbeth,* so the smaller, less pivotal role of Germont seemed to him too inconsequential to warrant his careful attention.

Verdi, never one to be swayed by public opinion, was unusually cavalier about the opera's failure. The day after the opening, he dashed off a series of short notes to friends and associates. His note to a former student, Emanuele Muzio, typifies his demeanor; "Dear Emanuele: "*Traviata* last night—a fiasco. Was it my fault or the singers'? . . . Time will tell."

There is an atypical lack of correspondence from Verdi about the whole matter. The opera, originally written as a contemporary drama, was set in the early 1700s for the Venice production—an alteration that Verdi would usually not have tolerated. Also, he had never been complacent about casting problems before, vehemently fighting for his rights to cast the first performances of his works and even cancelling them if his wishes were not followed.

Whatever the reasons for his casual approach, *La Traviata* was simply shelved for a year, until Verdi was approached by a Signor Gallo, a violinist from Venice whose family owned a respected theatre there, the Teatro San Benedetto. He had enjoyed the opera and wanted to stage a revival at the smaller theater. On May 6, 1854, 14 months after its disastrous premiere, *La Traviata* took the stage again to tremendous acclaim. Verdi mused that it was the same opera heard by the same public, and there was no accounting for the radical shift in their response. Like so many of its predecessors, it overcame a nightmarish premiere, was soon heard in all the world's major opera houses, and has remained an indispensable part of the standard repertoire to this day.

Perhaps both the opera's initial failure and ultimate success are due in part to the scandalous subject matter. Violetta, a beautiful young courtesan, abandons her lavish Parisian lifestyle for the true love of Alfredo, a penniless young

DRESS REHEARSAL,
GLYNDEBOURNE FESTIVAL OPERA

man from Provence. They are blissfully happy until his father intervenes, demanding that Violetta break off the relationship, because the fiancé of the young man's sister will not marry her while her brother's illicit union continues. Violetta agrees and sacrifices the idyllic relationship, telling Alfredo she no longer loves him. She returns to her empty life in Paris. In the end, alone and dying of tuberculosis, Violetta awaits Alfredo's return. His father tells him about her noble gesture, and Alfredo comes to be reunited with her. His appearance gives her the hope of recovery, but it is too late, and she dies in his arms.

The Italian operatic audience was accustomed to seeing human tribulation padded by the trappings of historical distance. The immediacy of presenting a modern French courtesan as a sympathetic character, whose nobility of spirit made her sacrifice her only chance at real happiness for the sake of her lover's family, was seen as an affront to the social mores of the time. Yet this same scenario was seen as vindication by those ostracized because of their lifestyles, and they rallied around the work. Verdi, who at this time was still "living in sin" with Strepponi, was one of them.

The great Giuseppe Verdi, who had for many years subtly reflected the political injustices of his homeland in his operas, now appeared to be taking on the whole social order of his time.

CHRISTINE NILSSON AS VIOLETTA

ACT I

Violetta Valéry, a young and beautiful courtesan, is receiving guests at a lavish party at her beautiful Paris home. She warmly greets her dearest friend, Flora, and her escort, the Marquis, who express concern about her capacity to host such a party, as she has recently been quite ill. Violetta responds with her personal philosophy, saying that she gives her life over to pleasure, and that pleasure is the best medicine for her ills.

ALFREDO GERMONT (BENIAMINO PRIOR) DURING THE INFAMOUS DRINKING SONG, SAN FRANCISCO OPERA, 1980

Another friend, Viscount Gaston de Letorieres, enters with a friend, Alfredo Germont, a young man from Provence. Gaston introduces Alfredo to Violetta, telling her that the young man has long been an admirer. Violetta greets him warmly. After asking a servant if dinner prepared, she calls on all to be seated and join in a toast. Gaston tells Violetta that during her recent illness Alfredo came to her home daily to inquire about her well-being. She is incredulous, but Gaston assures her it is true. She seeks verification from Alfredo, who admits it is true. She then teases her escort, the Baron Douphal, saying that he was nowhere near as attentive. The Baron replies that he has only known her a year, and Flora chides him for his response. The Baron then confides to Flora that he is developing a dislike for Alfredo.

Gaston invites the Baron to propose a toast, but he silently refuses. Everyone then begins coaxing Alfredo to propose a toast. He shyly asks Violetta if it would please her, and she responds that it would. Alfredo then begins a lively waltz song in praise of wine and pleasure, but especially in praise of love and the irresistible beauty of Violetta. She, in turn, sings that all, including love, is folly and that life's meaning is found in seeking pleasure.

They drink, and music is heard from an adjoining room. Violetta than invites her guests to go to the ballroom and dance. As they begin to leave the room Violetta rises to join them, but suddenly feels faint. Everyone gathers around her expressing concern, but she assures them that it is nothing and sends them in to dance, saying she will join them in a moment. All leave except Alfredo. Unaware that he is there, Violetta looks in a mirror and remarks at how pale she is. Alfredo chides her for her frivolous lifestyle, telling her she must take care of herself and that if she were his, he would take care of her. She responds that there is no one to care for her. Alfredo declares his love, but she dismisses it with a laugh. He is hurt by her response, and gradually she begins to understand that he is serious. They join in a duet in which Alfredo recounts the day he first saw her and how he has been in love with her ever since. She gently responds that she cannot love him or accept his love, that she can only offer him friendship and that he must find another love. She asks him to speak no more of love, and he replies that he will obey. She tenderly gives him a flower from her bosom, asking him to return it when it has withered. "Tomorrow?" he asks. "Yes," she replies. They gently say good-bye, and Alfredo kisses her hand and leaves.

CHORUS MEMBERS OF THE SAN FRANCISO OPERA CELEBRATE A FESTIVE EVENING,
ACT I

The guests reenter, noting that dawn is breaking and they must go. They all thank Violetta for her hospitality and gradually leave the house.

Alone, Violetta reflects on the profound affect Alfredo's declaration of love has had on her. Could this be what she has always longed for? Could she really escape her lonely and meaningless existence? But her pensive and hopeful mood changes abruptly. She declares that a meaningful love for her is folly, and she must continue to follow her frantic pursuit of pleasure until she dies. She stops short as she hears Alfredo's voice from under her balcony, repeating his ardent love for her. She momentarily reconsiders his sincerity, but quickly returns to her assertion that she must be always free and ends the Act in a florid affirmation of the lifestyle she has chosen.

ACT II

Scene 1

We are in the drawing room of the country home where Alfredo and Violetta have come to live together. Alfredo enters in hunting attire and pauses to reflect on the wonderful life he and Violetta have shared since she left the whirlwind of her social life in Paris three months before. Together, and unmindful of the world, they have created the perfect haven of love.

Their maid, Annina, enters, dressed for travel and clearly having just returned from a trip. Alfredo asks where she has been. Reluctantly, she tells him that Violetta sent her to Paris to arrange for the sale of her belongings to support their new life together. Filled with shame at his naiveté, Alfredo vows to go to Paris and secure the funds necessary to pay their mounting debts. He departs.

Violetta enters and asks Alfredo's whereabouts. Annina simply replies that he has gone to Paris and will return by evening. Another servant enters and delivers an invitation from Flora to a dance that evening. Violetta remarks that Flora will wait for her in vain.

The servant reenters to announce that a gentleman has arrived to see Violetta. She asks the servant to show the visitor in, and the servant presents

ALFREDO (BENIAMINO PRIOR) & VIOLETTA (VALERIE MASTERSON)

Giorgio Germont, Alfredo's father. She is startled, but graciously offers him a seat. After he sits, he rudely exclaims that his son's life is being ruined because of her. She responds indignantly and asks him to leave, but he tells her that his son plans to give her all his possessions. She tells him that can't be true and shows him the contract for the sale of all her goods. His brusque tone abates, and he asks how a woman capable of such nobility could have such a negative reputation. She replies that she loves Alfredo and has found happiness with him. She has made peace with her past, has repented and has been forgiven.

The elder Germont then tells her the reason for his visit. He tells her of Alfredo's sister and her impending marriage. Her fiancé, however, will not marry her unless Alfredo abandons his illicit affair and returns to his family. Violetta responds that to leave Alfredo for a time will be difficult, but she will do it. A brief separation, however, is not what Germont is requesting—he must ask her to give him up forever. Horrified, Violetta tells him that she cannot give Alfredo up, that she has no friends or family, and has given up everything for his love. She also confides that she has a deadly disease and hasn't long to live. Germont suggests that young men like his son are fickle, and

he may not always love her as he does now; since the union is not blessed by God, she may be left alone. Violetta reflects that her past sins will forever haunt her. Resigned, she tearfully tells Germont she will sacrifice the one precious thing in her life for his family's happiness. Germont comforts her, acknowledging her noble gesture and the quality of love she holds for Alfredo. He asks her if there is anything he can do for her, and she in turn asks that after her death Alfredo may know of the sacrifice she made for love of him. They bid each other farewell, and Germont retires to the garden outside.

VERDI, 1867

Violetta sits down, writes a farewell letter to her lover and seals it. Alfredo enters and startles her, asking to whom she is writing. She admits it was to him, but says he must read it later. He asks her if his father has come, telling her that he received a stern letter from him, but assuring her that the elder Germont will love her at first sight. She lies, telling Alfredo that his father has not come and

that she should not be there when he does. Alfredo should calm him first. Weeping, Violetta declares her love for Alfredo and begs him to express his love in return. Bidding him farewell, she leaves through the garden.

Confused by her demeanor, Alfredo absentmindedly reads a few lines from a book and then notices a man in the garden. A servant enters, telling him that Violetta has left with Annina. Shortly after, a messenger enters to deliver Violetta's farewell letter. Alfredo begins to read it and with a cry of despair, he turns to find his father at the door and throws himself into his arms. Germont tries to comfort him with a tender aria recalling the beauty of Provence, where the young man was raised. Germont implores Alfredo to return to his home and be a source

ALFREDO & GIORGIO GERMONT
AT FLORA'S PARTY, ACT II

of pride to his family again. Alfredo, who has been sitting with his face buried in his hands, suddenly looks up in a rage. He concludes it was Baron Douphol who stole Violetta from him and promises revenge. His father begs him to abandon this madness and return home. Alfredo sees the invitation from Flora on the table and is sure he will find Violetta there. In spite of his father's efforts to stop him, he storms from the room, determined to go to Paris and retrieve Violetta.

ACT II

Scene 2

In the lavish salon of Flora's Paris home, she is entertaining guests. She tells the Marquis that Alfredo and Violetta are coming, but he informs her they are separated and that Violetta will be coming with Baron Douphol. Dr. Grenvil expresses his surprise, as he had seen them only yesterday and they appeared happy. A brilliant entertainment ensues in which masked guests perform as gypsies and matadors. Flora and the Marquis tease one another about imagined infidelities, and all join in the good-natured banter.

Alfredo arrives, and the guests inquire as to Violetta's whereabouts. He nonchalantly responds that he doesn't know where she is. They then invite him to play cards, and he goes to the gaming table with Gaston and other guests to play.

Violetta enters on Baron Douphol's arm. He sees Alfredo, and taking Violetta aside, demands that she not say a single word to him. Disturbed by the tense scene, Violetta is taken aside by Flora and the Doctor who quietly ask what has happened.

ALFREDO (BENIAMINO PRIOR) SINGS OF HIS BROKEN HEART

Meanwhile, Alfredo is winning at cards. He loudly boasts that one unlucky in love is lucky at cards, and that his winnings will allow him to return to the country with the one who left him. The Baron challenges him to a game. Alfredo wins the first hand. Angrily, the Baron doubles the stakes. Alfredo wins again. The tension is broken by a servant announcing that dinner is served. Alfredo offers to continue the play, but the Baron answers that they will continue later. They all exit to the dining room.

Violetta quickly returns. She has asked Alfredo to come back to the salon so she can warn him against angering the Baron further. Alfredo enters the salon and disdainfully asks what Violetta wants. She tells him that she fears a duel, and if Alfredo should be killed, she would die. He arrogantly says he would cut the Baron down, and he asks her why she should care what happens to him. She begs him to leave. He responds that he will go only if she will follow. She confesses she has taken an oath not to stay with him. Alfredo demands to know who would make her take such an oath. Was it Douphol? Lying, Violetta answers, "Yes." Alfredo asks if she loves Douphol. Again, she lies, "Yes."

Infuriated, Alfredo runs to the door, calling all the guests back into the salon. They rush into the room, and Alfredo imperiously asks if they know this woman, who was once willing to sell all she had for love of him. He then declares that he will clear himself of the stain of this dishonor and repay what he owes her in full. He hurls his winnings at her feet. Humiliated, Violetta faints in Flora's arms.

The guests, horrified at Alfredo's actions, deride his insensitivity and demand that he leave at once. His father has arrived to witness the scene and expresses his contempt for his son's actions. Suddenly aware of what he has done, Alfredo comes to his senses and timidly expresses his remorse, arguing that he was driven to madness by the loss of his love. In a moving ensemble, all present express their various feelings: the Baron reviling Alfredo for his actions; the guests sympathizing with Violetta; and Germont, in an aside, reflecting on Violetta's virtue and faithfulness, about which only he truly knows. Violetta's voice soars above the ensemble as she expresses the hope that some day Alfredo will know the depth and breadth of her love for him. The Baron challenges Alfredo to a duel, and the remorseful young man is led away by his father.

ACT III

Violetta lies dying in her semi-darkened bedroom. Annina sits sleeping in a chair near her mistress's bed. Violetta awakens and requests some water, which Annina brings her. She then asks Annina to open the shutters. As she does, she sees Dr. Grenvil arriving in the street below. Violetta comments on what a faithful friend he has been and asks Annina's help in getting up to receive him. With difficulty, Annina helps Violetta to a nearby sofa, and upon entering, the doctor helps to make her comfortable.

He asks how she is feeling, and she responds that though she is suffering, she is at peace. The priest has been there to visit her, and he was most comforting. The doctor assures her that she will be feeling better soon. As he leaves, Annina asks about Violetta's condition, and the doctor tells her that she has only hours to live.

Annina returns to Violetta, offering encouragement. Violetta inquires if it is a holiday, and Annina tells her it is Carnival, and all of Paris is going mad. She then asks the maid how much money is left, and Annina replies they have 20 louis. Violetta instructs her to give ten to the poor, and when Annina suggests that won't leave them with much, Violetta assures her that it will be enough. She asks for her letters, then sends Annina away to make the donation.

Violetta opens a letter from Alfredo's father which she reads aloud. He tells her that the Baron was wounded in the duel, but is recovering. He also relates that Alfredo is abroad, but that he has been told of her sacrifice and is coming with his father to beg her forgiveness. The letter closes with his wishes for her happy future. It is, however, too late.

VIOLETTA
(MARIE
MCLAUGHLIN)
IN HER FINAL
MOMENTS

Violetta waits for Alfredo and his father, but they don't come. She looks in a mirror and sees how her disease has ravaged her. She mourns the loss of her happy love and says that her grave will be unmarked and unadorned by flowers or tears. She prays for God's forgiveness and desperately asks that she may come to Him.

As her soliloquy ends, Violetta hears the sound of revelers in the street. Annina enters and tries to keep her calm as she tells her that Alfredo is coming. He enters and they embrace ecstatically. He reaffirms his love and begs her forgiveness. She responds that there is nothing to forgive. Now they are together and nothing will separate them again. Alfredo paints an ideal picture of their future together. They will leave Paris for the country, they will make up for all their heartaches, her health will return and they will live together always in perfect bliss. In a euphoric trance, Violetta repeats his vision.

Strengthened by her joy, Violetta rises to her feet, saying they must go to church and give thanks for their reunion, but she falters and collapses into a chair. Alarmed, Alfredo supports her, but she attempts to rally again, asking Annina to bring her dress. Unable even to dress herself, Violetta falls back in defeat, cursing her weakness. In a panic, Alfredo sends Annina for the doctor and Violetta repeats the command, telling Annina to inform the doctor that her love has returned, and she must live again.

The maid leaves, and Violetta tells Alfredo that if his return cannot make her live, nothing can. As Alfredo attempts to calm her, she bewails the loss of her young life and all her hopes for happiness. Then Alfredo's father enters, and Violetta greets him warmly. He tells her he has come to welcome her as his daughter. But with a gentle embrace, she tells him it is too late. The doctor enters, and Violetta tells him she is dying in the presence of those she loves. Realizing that her death is imminent, Germont is stricken with remorse for having caused the separation of the two lovers.

Violetta then takes a small medallion from a drawer. It is a portrait of herself which she gives to Alfredo so that he may remember her. She tells him that he will love again, and when he does, he should give the medallion to his love and tell her that it is a portrait of one who is in heaven, praying for their happiness. As Violetta repeats these sentiments, all present pour out their grief over her impending death. Suddenly, there is a change in her demeanor. She rises and says the pain is gone, that she is reviving. She is overcome with joy. Then just as suddenly, she falls lifeless on the sofa. Dr. Grenvil rushes to check her condition and confirms that she is gone while Alfredo, Germont and Annina cry out in despair.

VIOLETTA & ALFREDO, REUNITED

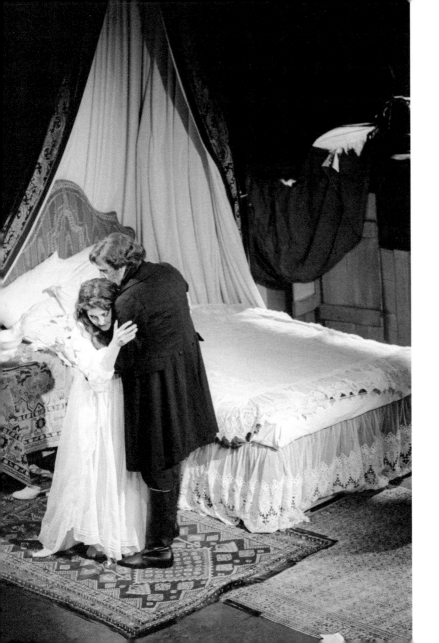

La Traviata

GIUSEPPE VERDI 1813-1901

Violetta Valéry...Beverly Sills
Alfredo Germont..Nicolai Gedda
Giorgio Germont...Rolando Panerai
Flora Bervoix...Delia Wallis
Annina..Mirella Fiorentini
Gastone..Keith Erwen
Barone Douphol..Terence Sharpe
Marchese d'Obigny..Richard Van Allan
Dottore Grenvil...Robert Lloyd
Giuseppe/Servant..Mario Carlin
Commissionario..William Elvin

Conducted by Aldo Ceccato
Royal Philharmonic Orchestra
The John Alldis Choir
Chorus Master: John Alldis

The Artists

⌒

BEVERLY SILLS (Violetta Valèry) is one of the most amazing personalities ever to grace the operatic stage. For 50 years her presence has been felt throughout the world of opera and beyond. Born Belle Silvermann in Brooklyn, she was a child star by the age of three and a fixture on New York radio until the age of twelve, when she "retired" to focus on her studies. These included Italian, French, and piano lessons, and voice lessons with the esteemed vocal pedagogue, Estelle Liebling. At the age of sixteen, Sills toured in operetta with the Schubert Opera Company, and a year later debuted with the Philadelphia Civic Opera and the esteemed San Francisco Opera Company.

In 1955 Sills joined the New York City Opera, achieving an early triumph in the New York premiere of Douglas Moore's *The Ballad of Baby Doe.* She continued with the company in leading roles, including all three heroines in Offenbach's *The Tales of Hoffman* in 1965. In 1966 she portrayed Cleopatra in Handel's *Giulio Cesare* to such unprecedented acclaim that it launched her international career.

In short order Sills conquered the operatic capitals of Europe, singing Mozart's Queen of the Night in *The Magic Flute* in Vienna, Pamira in Rossini's *The Siege of Corinth* at Milan's La Scala and the title role in Donizetti's *Lucia di*

BEVERLY SILLS AND HER DAUGHTER, WHO IS DEAF.

Lammermoor at Covent Garden. In the early 1970s, she sang all three of Donizetti's Tudor queens—*Maria Stuarda, Anna Bolena,* and *Elisabeth I* in *Roberto Deveraux* for her home company. These established her as one of the undisputed queens of bel canto in this century, and in 1975 she debuted at the Metropolitan Opera House as Pamira in Rossini's *The Siege of Corinth.*

Sills's repertoire encompasses more than 50 roles, from the Baroque rarity of Rameau's *Hippolyte et Aricie* to the twelve-tone intricacies of Nono's *Intolleranza*—and everything in between. One of her most famous portrayals was as Massenet's *Manon,* a work somewhat outside the mainstream of her standard fare. During her singing career she also did much to advance the cause of opera in America with her appearances on popular TV talk shows and in television specials, one of the most memorable of which paired her with the musical theater artist, Julie Andrews.

After retiring from the stage, Sills became General Director of the New York City Opera which she ran with distinction from 1979-89. Today she presides over the Board of Directors of Lincoln Center in New York, the premiere performing arts center in the nation. In 1980 she received the Presidential Medal of Freedom, and in 1985, a Kennedy Center Honor.

The role of Violetta holds a special place in Beverly Sills's heart. It was her first leading role as an aspiring young artist, one she performed countless times on tour, and it was also the vehicle for her successful debuts in Naples, Berlin and Venice. Early in life, she acquired the nickname "Bubbles," a name which reflects her ingratiating personality and a vocal quality which is so evident in this portrayal. Her unparalleled coloratura is dazzling in her first-act aria, *Sempre libera,* and the warmth of her second-act self-denial is heartrending. Her incredible acting skill is apparent in the careful handling of her third-act decline, in which the aria *Addio del passato* is particularly moving. In this recording we are treated to the broad vocal and dramatic range of one of the greatest ladies of the operatic stage.

NICOLAI GEDDA (Alfredo Germont) is widely regarded as having one of the most beautiful tenor voices of the century. He is frequently pointed to as the best possible model for young singers, who learn by listening to the integrity of his pitch, the beauty of his vocal lines and the ease of his technique. Also one of the most intelligent operatic artists of the century, he speaks and sings fluently in seven languages.

Gedda was born in Stockholm, the son of a Swedish mother and a Russian father. After leaving school he began a career in banking, but with the help of a client was able to begin vocal studies with the Swedish tenor, Carl Martin Oehman. After winning the Christine Nilsson Award, Gedda studied at the Royal Conservatory of Music in Stockholm.

He made his operatic debut in 1952 in *Le Postillon de Lonjumeau* at the Royal Opera House in Stockholm. Only months later, Gedda was hired to record the role of Dmitri the Pretender in Mussorgsky's *Boris Godunov,* and his future was secured. In 1953 he debuted at La Scala as Don Ottavio in Mozart's *Don Giovanni* and was chosen by Carl Orff to create the role of the groom in his *Il Trionfo di Afrodite.* Over the next two years he debuted at the Paris Opera and Covent Garden, and in 1957 he made his Metropolitan Opera debut, creating the role of Anatol in Samuel Barber's *Vanessa* in his first year there, and singing there regularly for over twenty years.

In 1964 he created the leading tenor role in the American premiere of Menotti's *The Last Savage,* and in 1965 he was given the title Court Singer to the Royal Court of Sweden, an honor conferred on less than 12 artists in 200 years.

SWEDISH TENOR NICOLAI GEDDA

The scope of Gedda's repertoire is unsurpassed, including over 200 works in the concert and operatic repertoire. He is equally at home as Lensky in Tchaikovsky's *Eugene Onegin* or singing an English folk song. His extensive discography includes almost 40 complete opera recordings in six languages, encompassing both lyric and dramatic roles and affording him the honor of being the most recorded tenor alive. He remains active today, mainly as a recitalist and in concert, and his recording career has continued into the 1990s.

The role of Alfredo is perfectly suited to Gedda's voice, and he is at his lyric best in this recording, handling the intimacy of *De miei bollenti spiriti* and the bravado of the frequently omitted second-act cabaletta with equal aplomb.

ROLANDO PANERAI (Giorgio Germont) was born in the small town of Campi Bisenzio near Florence. He pursued his vocal studies in Florence and Milan and made his debut in 1946 in Florence as Enrico Ashton in Donizetti's *Lucia di Lammermoor*. Over the following two years he appeared regularly in Naples where he debuted as Pharoah in Rossini's *Mose in Egitto*. In 1951 he made his La Scala debut as the high priest in Saint-Saens *Samson et Dalila*. He appeared there regularly for a number of years, singing such diverse roles as Appolo in Gluck's *Alceste* and the husband in Menotti's comedy, *Amelia al Ballo*. In 1957 he sang the title role in the Italian premiere of Hindemith's *Mathis der Maler* at La Scala, and in 1962 he created the title role in Turchi's *Il Buon Soldato Svejk* there.

Panerai's international career began in 1955 when he created the role of Ruprecht in Prokofiev's *The Flaming Angel* in Aix-en-Provence, where he also portrayed Mozart's Figaro. He debuted in Salzburg in 1957 as Ford in Verdi's *Falstaff,* and his American debut was with the San Francisco Opera in 1958, where he sang both the Rossini and Mozart Figaros and Marcello in Puccini's

La Bohème. His career has included all the major houses in Italy, Great Britain, France, Germany and the United States, including the Metropolitan Opera in New York. He remains active today; two of his latest specialties are the title roles in Verdi's *Falstaff* and Puccini's *Gianni Schicchi.*

Panerai's extensive discography includes over twenty complete operas, ranging from Mozart to Wagner in the German repertoire and from Rossini to Puccini in the Italian repertoire. Panerai's Germont is an intimate paternal figure which he portrays with a consistent richness of sound and intelligent characterization. He is the perfect father to Gedda's delicate and vital Alfredo, and with the elegance of Sills's Violetta, he masterfully rounds out an ideal cast for Verdi's masterpiece.

ALDO CECCATO (the conductor), is a native of Milan who began his musical career as a successful young pianist, equally comfortable in the classical and jazz genres. He studied at the Milan Conservatory and at Berlin's Hochschule fur Musik, where he conducted a student performance of Verdi's *Otello.* It was the concert in Milan where he conducted seven Vivaldi concerti that commanded the attention of the European musical establishment. He made his professional debut with *Don Giovanni* at Milan's Teatro Nuovo in 1964, and in 1966 he conducted the Italian premiere of Busoni's *Die Brautwahl* in Florence to critical acclaim. His early association with the famous Italian conductor-composer, Victor de Sabata, who admired the young conductor's interpretation of his tone poem *Juventu,* helped to establish demand for Ceccato's work.

His growing fame in Italy soon led to engagements in Germany, France, Britain and South America, and in 1969 Ceccato made his American debut at the Chicago Lyric Opera conducting Bellini's *I Puritani.* In 1970 he made his debut with the New York Philharmonic and went on to guest conduct all the major American orchestras. He also conquered all the major opera houses in Europe, guest conducting at Covent Garden, the Glyndebourne Festival and the Paris Opera, to name just a few. Since 1975, he has confined his activity primarily to Germany.

This *Traviata* is one of only two opera recordings under Ceccato's baton. He recorded Donizetti's *Maria Stuarda* also in 1971 and also with Beverly Sills. Known for his powerful leadership and attention to detail, Ceccato delivers an expansive reading of *La Traviata,* imbuing the genteel French setting with an unmistakably Verdian soul.

The Libretto

Act 1

PRELUDE

A drawing room in Violetta's home. In the background a door, opening to another room. There are two other lateral doors; to the left, a fireplace with a mirror over the mantel. In the centre of the room, a huge table richly laden. (Violetta is seated on a sofa, talking with Dr Grenvil and other friends. Some of her friends go to greet various guests as they arrive. Among them, the Baron and Flora, escorted by the Marquis.)

disk no. 1/track 1   The Prelude begins with a somber theme which represents the tragedy of Violetta's illness and early death. It is a theme we will hear again at the beginning of act III. This motive gives way to the theme of Violetta's farewell to Alfredo at the end of act II, scene 1. The melody is first stated by violins and cellos (01:47), then repeated by the cellos (02:50) with a violin obbligato or countermelody above it.

disk no. 1/track 2   The first scene opens with a lively theme that underscores the whole scene. This is real party music, reminiscent of the first scene of Verdi's previous opera, *Rigoletto*. The chorus speaks as one character throughout the opera, responding as one to the progressing action.

CORO I
Dell'invito trascorsa è già l'ora.
Voi tardaste.

CHORUS I
You were invited for an earlier hour.
You have come late.

CORO II
Giocammo da Flora, e giocando quell'ore volar.

VIOLETTA *(va loro incontro)*
Flora, amici, la notte che resta d'altre gioie qui fate brillar. Fra le tazze più viva è la festa.

FLORA, MARCHESE
E goder voi potrete?

VIOLETTA
Lo voglio;   al piacere m'affido, ed io soglio con tal farmaco i mali sopir.

TUTTI
Sì, la vita s'addoppia al gioir.

CHORUS II
We were playing cards at Flora's, and the time passed quickly.

VIOLETTA *(going to greet them)*
Flora, my friends, the rest of the evening will be gayer because you are here. Surely the evening is livelier with good food and drink?

FLORA, MARQUIS
And can you be lively?

VIOLETTA
I must be.
I give myself to pleasure, since pleasure is the best medicine for my ills.

ALL
Indeed, life is doubly heightened by pleasure.

(The Viscount Gastone de Letorières enters with Alfredo Germont. Servants are busily engaged at the table.)

GASTONE
In Alfredo Germont, o signora, ecco un altro che molto v'onora; pochi amici a lui simili sono.

VIOLETTA
(Violetta dà la mano ad Alfredo, che gliela bacia.)
Mio Visconte, mercé di tal dono.

MARCHESE
Caro Alfredo -

GASTONE
My dear Madam, in Alfredo Germont I present a man who greatly admires you; few friends are so fine as he.

VIOLETTA
(She offers her hand to Alfredo, who kisses it.)
My dear Viscount, thank you for this gift.

MARQUIS
My dear Alfredo -

ALFREDO
Marchese -

(They shake hands.)

GASTONE *(ad Alfredo)*
T'ho detto:
l'amistà qui s'intreccia al diletto.

(Meanwhile the servants have finished setting the table.)

VIOLETTA
Pronto è il tutto?
(Un servo fa cenno di sì.)
Miei cari, sedete:
è al convito che s'apre ogni cor.

TUTTI
Ben diceste - le cure segrete fuga sempre
l'amico licor.

(They take their places at the table. Violetta is seated between Alfredo and Gastone. Facing her Flora takes her place between the Marquis and the Baron. The remaining guests take their various places around the table. A moment of silence as the food is served. Violetta and Gastone are whispering to each other.)

È al convito che s'apre ogni cor.

GASTONE
Sempre Alfredo a voi pensa.

VIOLETTA
Scherzate?

ALFREDO
Marquis -

GASTONE *(to Alfredo)*
As I told you,
here friendship joins with pleasure.

VIOLETTA
Is everything ready?
(A servant nods in affirmation.)
Please be seated:
it is at table that the heart is gayest.

ALL
Well spoken - secret cares fly before that
great friend, wine.

It is at table that the heart is gayest.

GASTONE
Alfredo thinks of you always.

VIOLETTA
You are joking?

GASTONE
Egra foste, e ogni dì con affanno qui volò,
di voi chiese.

VIOLETTA
Cessate. Nulla son io per lui.

GASTONE
Non v'inganno.

VIOLETTA
Vero è dunque? Onde ciò?
Nol comprendo.

ALFREDO
Sì, egli è ver.

VIOLETTA
Le mie grazie vi rendo.
Voi, barone, non faceste altrettanto.

BARONE
Vi conosco da un anno soltanto.

VIOLETTA
Ed ei solo da qualche minuto.

FLORA (sottovoce al Barone)
Meglio fora se aveste taciuto.

BARONE (piano a Flora)
M'è increscioso quel giovin.

FLORA
Perché? A me invece simpatico egli è.

GASTONE
While you were ill, every day he called
to ask about you.

VIOLETTA
Don't talk like that. I am nothing to him.

GASTONE
I do not deceive you.

VIOLETTA
It is true then? But why?
I don't understand.

ALFREDO
Yes, it is true.

VIOLETTA
I thank you.
You, Baron, were less attentive.

BARON
I have only known you for a year.

VIOLETTA
And he for just a few minutes.

FLORA (in a low voice, to the Baron)
It would have been better to say nothing.

BARON (softly, to Flora)
I don't like this young man.

FLORA
Why not? I think he's very pleasant.

GASTONE *(ad Alfredo)*
E tu dunque non apri più bocca?

MARCHESE *(a Violetta)*
È a madama che scuoterlo tocca.

VIOLETTA
Sarò l'Ebe che versa.

ALFREDO
E ch'io bramo immortal come quella.

TUTTI
Beviamo.

GASTONE
O barone, né un verso, né un viva troverete
in quest'ora giuliva?

(The Baron shakes his head.)

Dunque a te -

(nodding to Alfredo)

TUTTI
Sì, sì, un brindisi.

ALFREDO
L'estro non m'arride.

GASTONE
E non sei tu maestro?

ALFREDO *(a Violetta)*
Vi fia grato?

GASTONE *(to Alfredo)*
And you have nothing more to say?

MARQUIS *(to Violetta)*
It's up to you to make him talk.

VIOLETTA
I shall be Hebe, the cup-bearer.

ALFREDO
And, like her, immortal, I hope.

ALL
Let us drink.

GASTONE
Baron - can't you find a toast for this happy
occasion?

Then it's up to you -

ALL
Yes, yes, a toast.

ALFREDO
Inspiration fails me.

GASTONE
But aren't you a master?

ALFREDO *(to Violetta)*
Would it please you?

VIOLETTA
Sì.

ALFREDO *(s'alza)*
Sì? L'ho già in cor.

MARCHESE
Dunque attenti!

TUTTI
Sì, attenti al cantor.

VIOLETTA
Yes.

ALFREDO *(rising)*
Yes? I have it already in my heart.

MARQUIS
Then - attention!

ALL
Yes, to the poet.

disc no. 1/track 3   *Libiamo* is one of the most famous "drinking songs" in the operatic repertoire. Its lusty waltz rhythm is a favorite of opera lovers, and it is frequently extracted and performed outside the opera.

ALFREDO
Libiamo, ne' lieti calici
che la bellezza infiora,
e la fuggevol ora
s'inebrii a voluttà.
Libiam ne' dolci fremiti
che suscita l'amore,
poiché quell'occhio al core
(indicando Violetta)
onnipotente va.
Libiamo amore, amor fra i calici
più caldi baci avrà.

TUTTI
Ah! Libiam, amor fra i calici
più caldi baci avrà.

VIOLETTA *(s'alza)*
Tra voi saprò dividere
il tempo mio giocondo;
tutto è follia nel mondo

ALFREDO
Drink from the joyful glass,
resplendent with beauty,
drink to the spirit of pleasure
which enchants the fleeting moment.
Drink to the thrilling sweetness
brought to us by love,
for these fair eyes, irresistibly,
(indicating Violetta)
pierce us to the heart.
Drink - for wine
will warm the kisses of love.

ALL
Drink - for wine
will warm the kisses of love.

VIOLETTA *(rising)*
I shall divide my gaiety
among you all;
Everything in life is folly,

REKNOWNED
SOPRANO MIRELLA
FRENI, AS VIOLETTA

ciò che non è piacer.
Godiam, fugace e rapido
è il gaudio dell'amore,
è un fior che nasce e muore,
né più si può goder.
Godiam, c'invita un fervido
accento lusinghier.

TUTTI
Ah! godiam, la tazza e il cantico
la notte abbella e il riso;
in questo paradiso
ne scopra il nuovo dì.

VIOLETTA *(ad Alfredo)*
La vita è nel tripudio.

ALFREDO *(a Violetta)*
Quando non s'ami ancora.

VIOLETTA
Nol dite a chi l'ignora.

ALFREDO
È il mio destin così.

TUTTI
Godiamo, la tazza e il cantico
la notte abbella e il riso;
in questo paradiso
ne scopra il nuovo dì.

(The sound of music is heard, coming from an adjoining room.)

Che è ciò?

except for pleasure.
Let us be joyful, for love
is a fleeting and short-lived joy.
A flower which blossoms and fades,
whose beauty is soon lost forever.
Be joyful - a caressing voice
invites us warmly to joy.

ALL
Ah! Be carefree - for wine and song
with laughter, embellish the night.
The new day breaking will find us still
in this happy paradise.

VIOLETTA *(to Alfredo)*
Life is only pleasure.

ALFREDO *(to Violetta)*
For those who don't know love.

VIOLETTA
Speak not of love to one who knows not
what it is.

ALFREDO
Such is my destiny.

ALL
Be carefree - for wine and song
with laughter, embellish the night.
The next day breaking will find us still
in this happy paradise.

What is that?

VIOLETTA
Non gradireste ora le danze?

TUTTI
Oh, il gentil pensier! Tutti accettiamo.

VIOLETTA
Usciamo dunque.

(As they are going out through the centre door, Violetta suddenly turns pale.)

Ohimè!

TUTTI
Che avete?

VIOLETTA
Nulla, nulla.

TUTTI
Che mai v'arresta?

VIOLETTA
Usciamo.

(She takes a few steps, but then is forced to stop again and to sit down.)

Oh Dio!

TUTTI
Ancora!

ALFREDO
Voi soffrite?

VIOLETTA
Wouldn't you like to dance now?

ALL
How kind of you! We accept with pleasure.

VIOLETTA
Let us go, then.

(As they are going out through the centre door, Violetta suddenly turns pale.)

Oh!

ALL
What is the matter?

VIOLETTA
Nothing, it is nothing.

ALL
Why have you stopped here?

VIOLETTA
Let us go out.

(She takes a few steps, but then is forced to stop again and to sit down.)

Oh God!

ALL
Again!

ALFREDO
Are you ill?

TUTTI
Oh ciel! Ch'è questo?

ALL
Heavens, what can it be?

VIOLETTA
Un tremito che provo.
Or là passate.

VIOLETTA
It's just a chill.
Go on - please - there.

(She points towards the other room.)

Fra poco anch'io sarò.

In just a few minutes I shall come -

TUTTI
Come bramate.

ALL
As you wish.

(All except Alfredo go into the other room.)

VIOLETTA *(Si alza e va a guardarsi allo specchio.)* Oh, qual pallor!

VIOLETTA *(looking into a mirror)*
How pale I am!

(turning she sees Alfredo)

Voi qui.

You are here!

ALFREDO
Cessata è l'ansia che vi turbò?

ALFREDO
Are you feeling better now?

VIOLETTA
Sto meglio.

VIOLETTA
Yes, better, thank you.

ALFREDO
Ah, in cotal guisa v'ucciderete - aver v'è d'uopo cura dell'esser vostro -

ALFREDO
Ah, this way you will kill yourself - you must take care of yourself -

VIOLETTA
E lo potrei?

VIOLETTA
But can I?

VIOLETTA & ALFREDO
(BENIAMINO PRIOR
& VALERIE MASTERSON)

ALFREDO
Oh, se mia
foste, custode io veglierei pe' vostri soavi dì.

VIOLETTA
Che dite? Ha forse alcuno
cura di me?

ALFREDO *(con passione)*
Perché nessuno al mondo v'ama.

VIOLETTA
Nessun?

ALFREDO
Tranne sol io.

VIOLETTA
Gli è vero. Sì grande amore dimenticato avea.

ALFREDO
Ridete? E in voi v'ha un core?

VIOLETTA
Un cor? sì, forse... e a che lo richiedete?

ALFREDO
Ah, se ciò fosse. Non potreste allora celiar.

VIOLETTA
Dite davvero?

ALFREDO
Io non v'inganno.

ALFREDO
If you were mine,
I should watch over you.

VIOLETTA
What are you saying? Is there anyone
to care for me?

ALFREDO *(passionately)*
That's because no one in the world loves
you -

VIOLETTA
No one?

ALFREDO
Except me.

VIOLETTA
It's true! I had forgotten this great love.

ALFREDO
You laugh? Have you no heart?

VIOLETTA
A heart? yes, perhaps - but why do you ask?

ALFREDO
Ah, if that were so, then you couldn't laugh
at me.

VIOLETTA
Are you serious?

ALFREDO
I do not deceive you.

VIOLETTA
Da molto è che mi amate?

VIOLETTA
Have you been in love with me for long?

disc no.1/track 5 *Un dì, felice, eterea.* The party atmosphere gives way to the more intimate mood of this famous duet in which Alfredo recalls his first sight of Violetta and rhapsodizes about his love for her. Soon (00:39) we hear the soaring theme that comes to represent their love and which is echoed throughout the opera.

ALFREDO
Ah, sì; da un anno.
Un dì felice, eterea,
mi balenaste innante,
e da quel dì tremante
vissi d'ignoto amor,
di quell'amor ch'è palpito
dell'universo intero,
misterioso, altero,
croce e delizia al cor.

ALFREDO
Yes, for a year.
One day you passed before me,
happy and light as air,
and ever since that day,
even without knowing it, I loved you -
with that love which is the very breath
of the universe itself -
mysterious and noble,
both cross and ecstasy of the heart.

VIOLETTA
Ah, se ciò è ver, fuggitemi.
Solo amistade io v'offro:
amar non so, né soffro
un così eroico amore.
Io sono franca, ingenua;
altra cercar dovete;
non arduo troverete
dimenticarmi allor.

VIOLETTA
Ah, if this is true, then leave me -
I offer you only friendship:
I cannot love, nor can I accept
so heroic a love from you.
I am simple and frank.
You must find another.
It won't be hard, then,
for you to forget me.

ALFREDO
Ah, amore misterioso, altero,
croce e delizia al cor.

ALFREDO
Love mysterious and noble,
both cross and ecstasy of the heart.

VIOLETTA
Non arduo troverete dimenticarmi allor.

GASTONE *(sulla porta di mezzo)*
Ebben? Che diavol fate?

VIOLETTA
Si folleggiava.

GASTONE
Ah, ah! Sta ben - restate.

(He withdraws.)

VIOLETTA
Amor dunque non più.
Vi garba il patto?

ALFREDO
Io v'obbedisco. Parto.

VIOLETTA *(si toglie un fiore dal seno)*
A tal giungeste?
Prendete questo fiore.

ALFREDO
Perché?

VIOLETTA
Per riportarlo -

ALFREDO
Quando?

VIOLETTA
It won't be hard, then, for you to forget me.

GASTONE *(in the doorway)*
Well, now? What the devil are you doing?

VIOLETTA
We were joking.

GASTONE
Aha! Good! Please stay.

VIOLETTA
Then - no more love.
Do you accept the pact?

ALFREDO
I obey. I shall leave you.

VIOLETTA *(taking a flower from her bosom)*
It's like that, then?
Take this flower.

ALFREDO
Why?

VIOLETTA
You shall bring it back -

ALFREDO
When?

VIOLETTA
Quando sarà appassito.

ALFREDO
Oh! Ciel! Domani -

VIOLETTA
Ebben, domani.

ALFREDO *(prende con trasporto il fiore)*
Io son felice!

VIOLETTA
D'amarmi dite ancora?

ALFREDO *(per partire)*
Oh, quanto v'amo!

VIOLETTA
Partite?

ALFREDO *(torna a lei, le bacia la mano)*
Parto.

VIOLETTA
Addio.

ALFREDO
Di più non bramo.

ALFREDO, VIOLETTA
Addio. Addio.

VIOLETTA
When it has withered.

ALFREDO
Oh Heavens! Tomorrow.

VIOLETTA
Good, tomorrow.

ALFREDO *(joyously accepting the flower)*
I am happy!

VIOLETTA
Do you still think you love me?

ALFREDO *(about to leave)*
Oh, how much I love you!

VIOLETTA
You are leaving?

ALFREDO *(coming near her, kissing her hand)*
I am leaving.

VIOLETTA
Goodbye.

ALFREDO
I desire nothing more.

ALFREDO, VIOLETTA
Goodbye. Goodbye.

(Alfredo goes out as the other guests return to the drawing room, flushed from dancing.)

disc no.1/track 7 The dance is over, and the guests return to the salon to bid Violetta farewell. They are accompanied by an exhilarating theme in the orchestra which reflects the gaiety of the party.

TUTTI

Si ridesta in ciel l'aurora
e n'è forza di partire;
mercé a voi, gentil signora,
di sì splendido gioir.
La città di feste è piena,
volge il tempo dei piacer;
nel riposo ancor la lena
si ritempri per goder.

ALL

Dawn is breaking in the sky
and we must leave.
Thank you, gentle lady,
for this delightful evening.
The city is filled with parties,
the season of pleasure is at its height.
We shall sleep now, to regain our strength
for another night of joy.

(They go out.)

disc no.1/track 8 Alone, Violetta muses on Alfredo's expressions of love. This begins a scene lasting twelve and a half minutes—a real tour de force for the solo soprano on stage.

VIOLETTA *(sola)*

È strano! È strano! In core
scolpiti ho quegli accenti!
Saria per me sventura un serio amore?
Che risolvi, o turbata anima mia?
Null'uomo ancora t'accendeva - O gioia
ch'io non conobbi, esser amata amando!
E sdegnarla poss'io
per l'aride follie del viver mio?

VIOLETTA *(alone)*

How strange! How strange! His words
are burned upon my heart!
Would a real love be a tragedy for me?
What decision are you taking, oh my soul?
No man has ever made me fall in love.
What joy, such as I have never known -
loving, being loved!
And can I scorn it
for the arid nonsense of my present life?

disc no.1/track 9 *Ah, fors'e lui,* is an extremely well-known and masterfully constructed aria. It begins with halting phrases in a minor key as Violetta reflects on her strange reaction to Alfredo's confession of love. This changes to an expansive, major key reminiscence of Alfredo's words and music. The process is repeated in a second verse.

Ah, fors'è lui che l'anima
solinga ne' tumulti
godea sovente pingere
de' suoi colori occulti!
Lui che modesto e vigile
all'egre soglie ascese,
e nuova febbre accese,
destandomi all'amor.
A quell'amor ch'è palpito
dell'universo intero,
misterioso, altero,
croce e delizia al cor!

Ah, perhaps he is the one
whom my soul,
lonely in the tumult, loved
to imagine in secrecy!
Watchful though I never knew it,
he came here while I lay sick,
awakening a new fever,
the fever of love,
of love which is the very breath
of the universe itself -
Mysterious and noble,
both cross and ecstasy of the heart.

disc no.1/track 10 *Follie! Follie!* In a sudden change of mood, Violetta escapes her reverie and reasserts her preference for her gay lifestyle. The orchestra skips along with her as what is mainly a role for lyric soprano becomes a coloratura showpiece.

Follie! follie! Delirio vano è questo!
Povera donna, sola,
abbandonata in questo
popoloso deserto
che appellano Parigi. Che spero or più?
Che far degg'io? Gioire,
di voluttà ne' vortici perir.
Gioir, gioir!

Folly! All is folly! This is mad delirium!
A poor woman, alone, lost in this
crowded desert which is known to men as
Paris. What can I hope for?
What should I do? Revel
in the whirlpool of earthly pleasures.
Revel in joy! Ah!

disc no.1/track 11 *Sempre libera* ("Forever free"). Violetta defines her creed in this most famous cabaletta. (The term is derived from the Italian word, cavallo, meaning "horse," and the music gallops along appropriately.) In an interesting dramatic effect, Alfredo's voice is heard from outside, declaring again his love for her (00:59), but Violetta will not be swayed. Her declaration of independence brings the act to a close with a stunning penultimate E-flat above high C—a note not written by Verdi, but a modern embellishment expected by most modern listeners.

Sempre libera degg'io
folleggiare di gioia in gioia,
vo' che scorra il viver mio
pei sentieri del piacer.
Nasca il giorno, o il giorno muoia,
sempre lieta ne' ritrovi,
a diletti sempre nuovi
dee volare il mio pensier.

ALFREDO (sotto al balcone)
Amore, amor è palpito...

VIOLETTA
Oh!

ALFREDO
...dell'universo intero -

VIOLETTA
Oh amore.

ALFREDO
Misterioso, misterioso, altero,
croce, croce e delizia,
croce e delizia, delizia al cor.

VIOLETTA
Follie! follie! Ah sì! Gioir, gioir!
Sempre libera degg'io
folleggiare di gioia in gioia,
vo' che scorra il viver mio
pei sentieri del piacer.
Nasca il giorno, o il giorno muoia,
sempre lieta ne' ritrovi,
a diletti sempre nuovi,
dee volare il mio pensier.

Forever free, I must pass
madly from joy to joy.
My life's course shall be
forever in the paths of pleasure.
Whether it be dawn or dusk,
I must always live. Ah!
Gaily in the world's gay places,
ever seeking newer joys.

ALFREDO (outdoors, under the balcony)
Love is the very breath...

VIOLETTA
Oh!

ALFREDO
...of the universe itself -

VIOLETTA
Love.

ALFREDO
Mysterious and noble,
both cross and ecstasy,
cross and ecstasy of the heart.

VIOLETTA
Folly! Folly! Ah yes! From joy to joy,
forever free, I must pass
madly from joy to joy.
My life's course shall be
forever in the paths of pleasure.
Whether it be dawn or dusk,
I must always live. Ah!
Gaily in the world's gay places,
ever seeking newer joys, etc.

ALFREDO

Amor è palpito
dell'universo -

VIOLETTA

Ah! Dee volar il mio pensier.
Ah! il mio pensier. Il mio pensier.

ALFREDO

Love is the very breath
of the universe itself.

VIOLETTA

Oh! My thoughts have to seek new joys.
Oh! My thoughts. My thoughts.

Act 2

SCENE ONE

A country house near Paris. A drawing room on the ground floor. In the background, facing the audience, there is a fireplace; on the mantelpiece, a clock and above it a mirror. On either side of the fireplace, French doors open on a garden. On the floor above, two other doors, facing each other. Chairs, tables, books, writing materials.

(Alfredo enters in hunting clothes.)

disc no. 1/track 12   The second act begins in the idyllic setting of Alfredo and Violetta's country hideaway. The vigorous introduction in the strings describes the joy of the young lovers in their new life together.

disc no. 1/track 13   De miei bollenti spiriti is another famous aria which frequently finds its way to the concert stage. Accompanied by energetic pizzicato strings, Alfredo pours out his youthful, ardent euphoria.

ALFREDO *(depone il fucile)*
Lunge da lei per me non v'ha diletto!
Volaron già tre lune
dacché la mia Violetta
agi per me lasciò, dovizie, amori
e le pompose feste ov'agli omaggi avvezza,
vedea schiavo ciascun di sua bellezza.
Ed or contenta in questi ameni luoghi
tutto scorda per me. Qui presso
a lei io rinascer mi sento.
E dal soffio d'amor rigenerato
scordo ne' gaudi suoi tutto il passato.
De' miei bollenti spiriti
il giovanile ardore
ella temprò col placido sorriso dell'amor!
Dal dì che disse: Vivere
io voglio a te fedel, ah, sì
dell'universo immemore,
io vivo quasi in ciel.

ALFREDO *(putting down his shotgun)*
I have no joy in life when she is far away!
Three months have passed
since Violetta gave up for me
a life of ease, luxury, love affairs
and the pomp of society, where, surrounded by adoration, she enslaved all with her beauty. Now, happy in this quiet country home, she has forgotten everything for me. And here, near her, I feel like a man reborn; invigorated by the pulse of love, I have forgotten the past in the joy of being with her. The violent fire of my youthful spirits was tempered by the quiet smile of her love!
Ever since the day when she said:
"I want to live only for you"
I seem to live in heaven,
unmindful of the world.

(Annina enters, dressed for travelling.)

disc no.1/track 14. As Alfredo grills Annina regarding the reasons for her trip to Paris, he is accompanied by agitated figures in the strings.

ALFREDO
Annina, donde vieni?

ALFREDO
Annina, where have you come from?

ANNINA
Da Parigi.

ANNINA
From Paris.

ALFREDO
Chi tel commise?

ALFREDO
Who sent you?

ANNINA
Fu la mia signora.

ANNINA
My mistress.

ALFREDO
Perché?

ANNINA
Per alienar cavalli, cocchi,
e quanto ancor possiede.

ALFREDO
Che mai sento!

ANNINA
Lo spendio è grande a viver qui solinghi.

ALFREDO
E tacevi?

ANNINA
Mi fu il silenzio imposto.

ALFREDO
Imposto? Or v'abbisogna?

ANNINA
Mille luigi.

ALFREDO
Or vanne - andrò a Parigi.
Questo colloquio non sappia la signora.
Il tutto valgo a riparare ancora.

(He leaves. Soon Violetta enters with various papers in her hand. She speaks with Annina.)

VIOLETTA
Alfredo?

ALFREDO
Why?

ANNINA
To take the horses, the carriages,
and whatever else is hers.

ALFREDO
What is this!

ANNINA
It is very expensive, living here all alone.

ALFREDO
What are you hiding from me?

ANNINA
I was sworn to silence.

ALFREDO
Sworn! Tell me, how much is needed?

ANNINA
A thousand louis.

ALFREDO
Go now - I shall go to Paris.
Madam must know nothing of our talk.
I can still take care of everything.

VIOLETTA
Alfredo?

ANNINA
Per Parigi or or partiva.

VIOLETTA
E tornerà?

ANNINA
Pria che tramonti il giorno -
dirvel m'impose -

VIOLETTA
È strano!

ANNINA (*presentandole una lettera*)
Per voi.

VIOLETTA (*prendendola*)
Sta ben. In breve
giungerà un uom d'affari -
entri all'istante.

(Violetta, reading the letter)

Ah, ah! Scopriva Flora il mio ritiro.
E m'invita a danzar per questa sera!
Invan m'aspetterà.

ANNINA
È qui un signore.

VIOLETTA
Sarà lui che attendo.

ANNINA
He has just left for Paris.

VIOLETTA
When will he come back?

ANNINA
Before evening.
He asked me to tell you.

VIOLETTA
How strange!

ANNINA (*handing her a letter*)
For you.

VIOLETTA (*taking it*)
Good. In a few minutes a man is coming
on business.
Show him in immediately.

Aha! Flora has found my hideaway!
She has invited me to a dance this evening!
She'll wait for me in vain.

ANNINA
A gentleman to see you.

VIOLETTA
It must be the man I'm expecting.

(She gestures for Annina to admit him. Giorgio Germont enters.)

ALFREDO (WALTER MACNEIL), DISTRAUGHT
OVER VIOLETTA'S SUDDEN DEPARTURE

GERMONT
Madamigella Valéry?

VIOLETTA
Son io.

GERMONT
D'Alfredo il padre in me vedete!

VIOLETTA

(Surprised, she offers him a chair.)

Voi!

GERMONT
Sì, dell'incauto, che a ruina corre,
ammaliato da voi.

VIOLETTA *(risentita, alzandosi)*
Donna son io, signore, ed in mia casa;
ch'io vi lasci assentite
più per voi che per me.

(She is on the point of going out.)

GERMONT
(Quai modi!) Pure -
disc no. 1/track 23
VIOLETTA
Tratto in error voi foste.

GERMONT
De' suoi beni egli dono vuol farvi.

GERMONT
Mademoiselle Valéry?

VIOLETTA
Yes.

GERMONT
I am Alfredo's father!

VIOLETTA

You!

GERMONT
Yes, father of this reckless lad, who is
rushing to his ruin because of you.

VIOLETTA *(rising, with resentment)*
I, sir, am a woman and in my own home.
Now please excuse me,
more for your sake than for mine.

GERMONT
(What spirit!) And yet -

VIOLETTA
You have been badly advised.

GERMONT
He wants to give you all his possessions.

VIOLETTA
Non l'osò finora - rifiuterei.

GERMONT (*guardando intorno*)
Pur tanto lusso -

VIOLETTA
A tutti è mistero quest'atto.
A voi nol sia.

(*She gives him the paper.*)

GERMONT (*Germont scorre le carte.*)
Ciel! Che discopro!
D'ogni vostro avere or volete spogliarvi?
Ah, il passato, perché v'accusa?

VIOLETTA
Più non esiste - or amo Alfredo, e Dio
lo cancellò col pentimento mio.

GERMONT
Nobili sensi invero!
disc no. 2/track 1
VIOLETTA
Oh, come dolce mi suona il vostro accento!

GERMONT
Ed a tai sensi
un sacrifizio chieggo -

VIOLETTA (*alzandosi*)
Ah, no, tacete - terribil cosa chiedereste
certo.Il previdi - v'attesi - era
felice troppo.

VIOLETTA
So far, he hasn't dared - I should refuse.

GERMONT (*looking about him*)
Such luxury -

VIOLETTA
This paper is a secret from everyone.
But it shall not be from you.

GERMONT (*after looking at them briefly*)
Heavens! What is this!
You wish to sell everything you own?
Ah, why does your past accuse you so?

VIOLETTA
The past does not exist - I love Alfredo
now; God wiped out my past with my
repentance.

GERMONT
These are truly noble sentiments!

VIOLETTA
Ah, how good to hear these words from
you!

GERMONT
And in the name of these sentiments, I ask
a sacrifice -

VIOLETTA (*arising*)
Ah, no, do not say it. Certainly you would
ask some frightening thing.I knew it - I
expected you - I was too happy.

GERMONT
D'Alfredo il padre
la sorte, l'avvenir domanda or qui
de' suoi due figli.

VIOLETTA
Di due figli!

GERMONT
Alfredo's father
asks you to decide the fate
of his two children.

VIOLETTA
His two children!

disc no. 1/track 17 This piece is a cabaletta for tenor, frequently cut by at least half, if not altogether, because it tends to hold up the dramatic action. In this recording, it is restored in full and ends on a magnificent high C!

GERMONT
Sì!
Pura siccome un angelo
Iddio mi diè una figlia;
se Alfredo nega riedere
in seno alla famiglia,
l'amato e amante giovine
cui sposa andar dovea,
or si ricusa al vincolo
che lieti ne rendeva.
Deh, non mutate in triboli
le rose dell'amor.
A' prieghi miei resistere no, no
non voglia il vostro cor.

VIOLETTA
Ah, comprendo - dovrò per alcun tempo
da Alfredo allontanarmi - doloroso
fora per me - pur -

GERMONT
Non è ciò che chiedo.

GERMONT
Yes.
God blessed me with a daughter,
like an angel in her purity;
if Alfredo refuses to return
to the bosom of his family,
the young man in love and beloved in turn,
who was soon to marry my daughter,
would reject this bond
on which our happiness depends.
Ah, do not be the cause of love's roses
changing into thorns.
Do not let your heart refuse
what I so fervently ask of you. No! No!

VIOLETTA
Ah, I understand - I must leave Alfredo
for a time. It will be painful
for me - yet -

GERMONT
That is not what I ask.

VIOLETTA
Cielo, che più cercate?
Offersi assai!

GERMONT
Pur non basta.

VIOLETTA
Volete che per sempre a lui rinunzi?

GERMONT
È d'uopo!

VIOLETTA
Heaven, what more can you ask!
I offered much!

GERMONT
But not enough.

VIOLETTA
You want me to give him up forever?

GERMONT
You must!

disc no. 1/track 18 Alfredo's father enters the scene to an ominous theme in the low strings. A long duet ensues in which we gradually hear Germont's anger subside as his sympathy for Violetta's situation grows.

VIOLETTA
Ah no! - giammai! No, no!
Non sapete quale affetto
vivo, immenso m'arda in petto?
Che né amici, né parenti
io non conto tra' viventi?
E che Alfredo m'ha giurato
che in lui tutto troverò?
Non sapete che colpita
d'atro morbo è la mia vita?
Che già presso il fine vedo?
Ch'io mi separi da Alfredo!
Ah, il supplizio è sì spietato,
che a morir preferirò.

GERMONT
È grave il sacrifizio,
ma pur tranquilla uditemi,
bella voi siete e giovine -
col tempo -

VIOLETTA
No - never! No, no!
Can you not see what tremendous,
burning love I feel for him,
I, who have no friends or family
among the living?
Don't you know that Alfredo swore
that I should find everything in him?
Don't you know that my life
is endangered by a terrible disease,
that I have but a short time to live?
To leave Alfredo forever?
Ah, the anguish would be so cruel
that I should prefer to die.

GERMONT
The sacrifice is great,
but hear me out patiently.
You are still young and beautiful -
in time -

VIOLETTA
Ah, più non dite -
v'intendo - m'è impossibile.
Lui solo amar vogl'io.

GERMONT
Sia pure - ma volubile sovente è l'uom -

VIOLETTA
Gran Dio!

GERMONT
Un dì, quando le veneri
il tempo avrà fugate,
fia presto il tedio a sorgere -
che sarà allor? Pensate -
per voi non avran balsamo
i più soavi affetti,
poiché dal ciel non furono
tai nodi benedetti.

VIOLETTA
È vero! È vero!

GERMONT
Ah, dunque sperdasi tal sogno seduttore.

VIOLETTA
È vero! È vero!

GERMONT
Siate di mia famiglia l'angel consolatore
Violetta, deh, pensateci, ne siete in tempo
ancor. È Dio che ispira, o giovine,
tai detti a un genitor.

VIOLETTA
Ah, say nothing more.
I understand - I cannot -
I shall never love anyone but him.

GERMONT
That may well be - but men are often
fickle.

VIOLETTA
Oh God!

GERMONT
Once time has staled
the delights of love,
tedium will follow quickly.
Then what? Think -
Even the deepest feelings
can bring you no balm,
since this bond was never
blessed by heaven.

VIOLETTA
It's true! It's true!

GERMONT
Ah, then lay aside this beguiling dream.

VIOLETTA
It's true! It's true!

GERMONT
Be rather the consoling angel
of my family. Violetta. Think -
You still have time. Young lady, it is God
who inspiresthese words on a father's lips.

VIOLETTA
Così alla misera ch'è un dì caduta,
di più risorgere speranza è muta!
Se pur benefico le indulga Iddio,
l'uomo implacabil per lei sarà.

GERMONT
Siate di mia famiglia l'angiol consolator.

VIOLETTA *(poi, piangendo, a Germont)*
Ah! dite alla giovine sì bella e pura
ch'avvi una vittima della sventura,
cui resta un unico raggio di bene -
che a lei il sacrifica e che morrà!

GERMONT
Piangi, piangi, o misera, supremo, il veggo,
è il sacrifizio che ora ti chieggo.
Sento nell'anima già le tue pene;
coraggio e il nobile tuo cor vincerà!

VIOLETTA
Dite alla giovine sì bella e pura
ch'avvi una vittima della sventura,
cui resta un unico raggio di bene
che a lei il sacrifica e che morrà!

GERMONT
Ah supremo, il veggo,
è il sacrificio ch'ora ti chieggo.
Sento nell'anima già le tue pene;
coraggio e il nobile cor vincerà!
Piangi, o misera!

VIOLETTA
Imponete.

VIOLETTA
All hope of rising again is forever gone.
For the wretched woman who erred one
day! Even if God grants her mercy
charitably Man will always be implacable.

GERMONT
Be rather the consoling angel of my family.

VIOLETTA *(then, to Germont as she weeps)*
Oh, tell your daughter, so lovely and pure,
that a poor and wretched woman,
who has but one precious thing in life -
will sacrifice it for her - and then will die!

GERMONT
Weep, weep, poor girl. I see now
that the sacrifice I asked could not be
greater. Within my heart I feel what you
must suffer; be brave, your noble heart will
conquer all.

VIOLETTA
Tell your daughter, so lovely and pure,
that a poor and wretched woman,
who has but one precious thing in life -
will sacrifice it for her - and then will die!

GERMONT
I see now that the sacrificeI asked could
not be greater, within my heart I feel what
you must suffer, be brave, your noble heart
will conquer all.
Weep, poor girl.

VIOLETTA
Tell me what I must do.

GERMONT
Non amarlo ditegli.

VIOLETTA
Nol crederà.

GERMONT
Partite.

VIOLETTA
Seguirammi.

GERMONT
Allor -

VIOLETTA
Qual figlia m'abbracciate,
forte così sarò.

(They embrace.)

Tra breve ei vi fia reso.
Ma afflitto oltre ogni dire.

(pointing to the garden)

A suo conforto di colà volerete.

(Violetta sits down to write.)

GERMONT
Che pensate?

VIOLETTA
Sapendo, v'opporreste al pensier mio.

GERMONT
Tell him you don't love him.

VIOLETTA
He won't believe me.

GERMONT
Go away, then.

VIOLETTA
He will follow me.

GERMONT
Then -

VIOLETTA
Embrace me as if I were your daughter -
it will give me strength.

Soon he will be yours again,
but desperately sad.

Out there you will hurry to comfort him.

GERMONT
What is it?

VIOLETTA
If I told you, you would oppose my wish.

GERMONT
Generosa! E per voi che far poss'io?
O generosa!

VIOLETTA *(tornando a lui)*
Morrò! La mia memoria non fia ch'ei
maledica, se le mie pene orribili vi sia chi
almen gli dica.

GERMONT
No, generosa, vivere,
e lieta voi dovrete;
mercè di queste lagrime
dal cielo un giorno avrete.

VIOLETTA
Conosca il sacrifizio
ch'io consumai d'amore -
che sarà suo fin l'ultimo
sospiro del mio cor.

GERMONT
Premiato il sacrifizio
sarà del vostro core;
d'un'opra così nobile
sarete fiera allor. Sì, sì -

VIOLETTA
Conosca il sacrifizio
ch'io consumai d'amore -
che sarà suo fin l'ultimo
sospiro del mio cor.

GERMONT
Sarete fiera allor.
D'un'opra così nobile
sarete fiera allor.

GERMONT
Generous woman! What can I do for you?
Generous woman!

VIOLETTA *(returning near him)*
I shall die! Let him not curse my memory;
when I am dead, let someone tell him of
my suffering.

GERMONT
No, generous woman, you must live,
and live in happiness.
Heaven one day will recompense these
tears.

VIOLETTA
Let him know the sacrifice
which I made for love -
for the very last breath of life
will be for him alone.

GERMONT
And your heart's sacrifice
will be rewarded.
Then your heart will be proud
of so noble an act. Yes, yes, yes -

VIOLETTA
Let him know the sacrifice
which I made for love -
For the very last breath of life
will be for him alone.

GERMONT
Of so noble an act
then your heart will be proud
of so noble an act.

Premiato il sacrifizio
sarà del vostro cor;
d'un'opra così nobil
sarete fiera allor.

VIOLETTA
Qui giunge alcun! Partite!

GERMONT
Oh, grato v'è il cor mio!

VIOLETTA
Partite! Non ci vedrem più forse -

(They embrace.)

VIOLETTA, GERMONT
Siate felice!

VIOLETTA
Addio!

GERMONT
Addio!

VIOLETTA
Conosca il sacrifizio,

GERMONT
Sì!

VIOLETTA
...ch'io consumai d'amore -
che sarà suo fin l'ultimo...
Addio!

And your heart's sacrifice
will be rewarded.
Then your heart will be proud
of so noble an act.

VIOLETTA
Someone is coming...you must leave.

GERMONT
Oh, how grateful I am to you!

VIOLETTA
Leave me. We may never see each other
again.

VIOLETTA, GERMONT
May you be happy.

VIOLETTA
Goodbye!

GERMONT
Goodbye!

VIOLETTA
Let him know the sacrifice...

GERMONT
Yes.

VIOLETTA
...which I made for love...
...for the very last breath of life.
Goodbye!

GERMONT
Addio!

VIOLETTA
che sarà suo fin l'ultimo...
Addio!

VIOLETTA, GERMONT
Felice siate, addio!

(Germont goes out through the garden door.)

VIOLETTA
Dammi tu forza, o cielo!

(She sits down and writes, then rings for the servant..Annina enters.)

ANNINA
Mi richiedeste?

VIOLETTA
Sì, reca tu stessa questo foglio -

(Annina reads the address, then looks up in surprise.)

Silenzìo - va' all'istante.

(Annina goes out.)

Ed or si scriva a lui.
Che gli dirò? Chi men darà il coraggio?

(She writes, then seals the letter.)

ALFREDO *(Entra.)*
Che fai?

GERMONT
Goodbye!

VIOLETTA
...for the very last breath of life.
Goodbye!

VIOLETTA, GERMONT
May you be happy...goodbye!

VIOLETTA
Give me strength, oh Heaven!

ANNINA
You rang for me?

VIOLETTA
Yes, please deliver this letter yourself.

Silence - go immediately.

And now to write to him.
What can I say? Who will give me courage?

ALFREDO *(entering)*
What are you doing?

VIOLETTA

(concealing the letter)

Nulla.

ALFREDO
Scrivevi?

VIOLETTA
Sì - no -

ALFREDO
Qual turbamento! A chi scrivevi?

VIOLETTA
A te -

ALFREDO
Dammi quel foglio.

VIOLETTA
No, per ora.

ALFREDO
Mi perdona - son io preoccupato -

VIOLETTA
Che fu?

ALFREDO
Giunse mio padre -

VIOLETTA
Lo vedesti?

VIOLETTA

Nothing.

ALFREDO
You were writing?

VIOLETTA
Yes - no -

ALFREDO
But what confusion! To whom were you writing?

VIOLETTA
To you -

ALFREDO
Give me the letter.

VIOLETTA
No, not now.

ALFREDO
Forgive me - I am concerned about -

VIOLETTA
What has happened?

ALFREDO
My father was here.

VIOLETTA
Did you see him?

ALFREDO
Ah, no: severo scritto mi lasciava.
Però l'attendo, t'amerà in vederti.

VIOLETTA
Ch'ei qui non mi sorprenda,
lascia che m'allontani - tu lo calma -
ai piedi suoi mi getterò -
divisi ei più non ne vorrà -
sarem felici -
perché tu m'ami, Alfredo, non è vero?

ALFREDO
Oh, quanto! Perché piangi?

VIOLETTA
Di lagrime aveva d'uopo -
or son tranquilla -
lo vedi? Ti sorrido - lo vedi?
Sarò là tra quei fior presso a te sempre.
Amami, Alfredo, quant'io t'amo.
Addio!

ALFREDO
Ah, no. He left a stern letter for me.
But I'm expecting him. He'll love you at
first sight.

VIOLETTA
He must not find me here.
Let me go away - you calm him -
I'll throw myself at his feet - then
he'll not want to separate us. We shall be
happy - because you love me, you love me
Alfredo, you love me, don't you?

ALFREDO
So much! Why are you weeping?

VIOLETTA
I needed tears -
now I feel better -
See? I am smiling at you - see?
I shall always be here, near you, among the
flowers.
Love me, Alfredo, love me as much as I
love you.
Goodbye!

(She runs out into the garden.)

Alone, to the plaintive accompaniment of a solo clarinet, Violetta writes her farewell
to her lover.

Disc 2

ALFREDO
Ah, vive sol quel core all'amor mio!

ALFREDO
Ah, this dear one lives only for my love!

*(He sits down, reads a book for a moment. Then he stands up and goes to look at
the clock on the mantel.)*

È tardi; ed oggi forse
più non verrà mio padre.

It is late: perhaps today
my father will not come.

(Alfredo's father is seen at a distance, crossing thegarden.)

Qualcuno è nel giardino!
Chi è là?

Someone is in the garden!
Who is it?

(He is on the point of going out.)

COMMISSIONARIO
Il signor Germont?

MESSENGER
Signor Germont?

ALFREDO
Son io.

ALFREDO
I am he.

COMMISSIONARIO
Una dama
da un cocchio, per voi, di qua non lunge,
mi diede questo scritto.

MESSENGER
A lady in a carriage, not far down the road,
gave me this letter.

(He gives the letter to Alfredo, who tips him.)

ALFREDO
Di Violetta! Perché son io commosso!
A raggiungerla forse ella m'invita -
Io tremo! Oh ciel! Coraggio!

ALFREDO
From Violetta! Why am I so upset?
Perhaps she wants me to join her -
I am trembling. Oh, Heaven! Courage!

(He opens the letter and reads:)

"Alfredo, al giungervi di questo foglio..."

"Alfredo, by the time you receive this
letter"

(thunderstruck, he cries out:)

Ah!

Ah!

(Turning, he sees his father, and throws himself into his arms.)

Padre mio!	Father!

GERMONT
Mio figlio!
Oh, quanto soffri! Oh, tergi il pianto -
ritorna di tuo padre orgoglio e vanto.

GERMONT
My son!
Oh, how you are suffering!
Ah, dry your tears -be once again your
father's pride.

(In despair, Alfredo sits down at the table, his head in his hands.)

disc no. 1/track 24   Alfredo enters, and over an agitated figure in the orchestra, he questions Violetta about the letter. The tension continues (00:40) as she asks him to meet his father after she has gone. At the piece's climax (01:40), we hear the expansive theme we heard in the Prelude over tremolo strings.

Di Provenza il mar, il suol
chi dal cor ti cancellò?
Al natio fulgente sol qual destino ti furò?
Oh, rammenta pur nel duol
ch'ivi gioia a te brillò;
e che pace colà sol
su te splendere ancor può.
Dio mi guidò!
Ah! il tuo vecchio genitor
tu non sai quanto soffrì.
Te lontano, di squallor
il suo tetto si coprì,
ma se alfin ti trovo ancor,
se in me speme non fallì,
se la voce dell'onor
in te appien non ammutì,
Dio m'esaudì!
Né rispondi d'un padre all'affetto?

The sea, the hills of Provence,
who effaced them from your heart?
What destiny took you away
from the sunny land of your birth?
Oh, remember in your sorrow
what joy warmed you there;
and that only there can your soul find
peace again.
God brought me here!
Ah! You cannot know how your old father
has suffered.
With you away his house is clouded with
sorrow. But at last I have found you,
if my hope has not been in vain.
If the voice of honour is not wholly stilled
in you. But I have found you again.
God has answered my prayer!
Don't you return your father's love?

ALFREDO	**ALFREDO**

(Suddenly he sees Flora's letter on the table and exclaims:)

Ah! ell'è alla festa!	Ah! She is at the party! Let me fly
Volisi l'offesa a vendicar.	to take revenge for this offence.

GERMONT	**GERMONT**
Che dici! Ah, ferma!	What are you saying? Stop!

(Alfredo runs out of the house, followed by his father.)

SCENE TWO

A salon in Flora's home, richly furnished and brightly lighted. A door to the rear, others on either side. To the right, somewhat to the foreground, a gaming table with equipment for play; left, an elaborate table with flowers and refreshments; nearby, sofa and chairs.

(Flora, the Marquis and Dr. Grenvil enter with other guests -all chatting.)

Di Provenza il mar il suol is one of the most outstanding baritone arias in the repertoire. The opening theme, played by woodwinds in thirds, has a folk-like quality which describes the rural setting that was Alfredo's childhood home.

FLORA	**FLORA**
Avrem lieta di maschere la notte:	Later we shall be entertained by masks:
n'è duce il viscontino -	the Viscount is in charge.
Violetta ed Alfredo anco invitai.	I've invited Violetta and Alfredo.

MARCHESE	**MARQUIS**
La novità ignorate?	Haven't you heard the news?
Violetta e Germont sono disgiunti.	Violetta and Germont have separated.

DOTTORE, FLORA Fia vero?	**DOCTOR, FLORA** Have they really?
MARCHESE Ella verrà qui col barone.	**MARQUIS** She is coming with the Baron.
DOTTORE Li vidi ieri ancor - parean felici.	**DOCTOR** I saw them only yesterday - they looked happy.

(The sound of laughing voices is heard.)

FLORA Silenzio - udite?	**FLORA** Silence - do you hear?
FLORA, DOTTORE, MARCHESE Giungono gli amici.	**FLORA, DOCTOR, MARQUIS** Our friends are coming.

(Ladies disguised as gypsies enter.)

ZINGARE Noi siamo zingarelle venute da lontano; d'ognuno sulla mano leggiamo l'avvenir. Se consultiam le stelle null'avvi a noi d'oscuro, e i casi del futuro possiamo altrui predir. Vediamo -	**GYPSIES** We are gypsies. come from afar; the fortunes of all we can read in their hands. When we call upon the stars, nothing is hidden from us, and we can tell you all what the future holds in store. Let us see -
CORO I *(osservando la mano di Flora)* Voi, signora, rivali alquante avete.	**CHORUS I** *(examining Flora's palm)* You, Madam, have many rivals.
CORO II *(osservando la mano del Marchese)* Marchese, voi non siete model di fedeltà.	**CHORUS II** *(examining the Marquis's palm)* Marquis, you are scarcely a model of fidelity.

FLORA *(al Marchese)*
Fate il galante ancora?
Ben, vo' me la paghiate -

MARCHESE
Che diamin vi pensate?
L'accusa è falsità.

FLORA
La volpe lascia il pelo,
non abbandona il vizio.
Marchese mio, giudizio,
o vi farò pentir.

TUTTI
Su via, si stenda un velo
sui fatti del passato;
già quel ch'è stato è stato,
badiamo/badate all'avvenir.

FLORA *(to the Marquis)*
So you still play the gallant?
Fine - I'll make you pay for this.

MARQUIS
What the devil are you thinking?
It's a bare-faced lie.

FLORA
The fox may lose his brush,
but never abandons his rascality.
Take care, my dear Marquis,
or you'll be sorry, I swear.

ALL
Come, come, whatever's happened
shall be veiled by the past;
what's been has been,
think only of what's to be.

(Flora and the Marquis shake hands. Now from the right, Gastone and other men, dressed as Spanish matadors and picadors, enter.)

GASTONE, MATTADORI
Di Madride noi siam mattadori,
siamo i prodi del circo dei tori,
testé giunti a godere del chiasso
che a Parigi si fa pel Bue grasso;
È una storia se udire vorrete,
quali amanti noi siamo saprete.

GLI ALTRI
Sì, sì, bravi; narrate, narrate:
con piacere l'udremo.

GASTONE, MATTADORI
Ascoltate.

GASTONE, MATADORS
We're matadors, from Madrid,
the champions of the bullring.
We've just arrived to join in the fun
of carnival time in Paris;
if you'll hear our story to the end,
you'll know what great lovers we are.

THE OTHERS
Yes, yes, good! Tell us, tell us:
we'll hear your story with pleasure.

GASTONE, MATADORS
Listen, then.

È Piquillo un bel gagliardo
biscaglino mattador:
forte il braccio, fiero il guardo
delle giostre egli è signor.
D'Andalusa giovinetta
follemente innamorò;
ma la bella ritrosetta
così al giovane parlò:
"Cinque tori in un sol giorno
vo' vederti ad atterrar;
e, se vinci, al tuo ritorno
mano e cor ti vo' donar."
Sì, gli disse, e il mattadore,
alle giostre mosse il piè;
cinque tori, vincitore,
sull'arena egli stendé.

GLI ALTRI
Bravo, bravo il mattadore,
ben gagliardo si mostrò,
se alla giovane l'amore
in tal guisa egli provò!

GASTONE, MATTADORI
Poi, tra plausi, ritornato
alla bella del suo cor,
colse il premio desiato
tra le braccia dell'amor.

GLI ALTRI
Con tai prove i mattadori
san le belle conquistar!

GASTONE, MATTADORI
Ma qui son più miti i cori;
a noi basta folleggiar.

Piquillo is a strapping young man.
A matador from Biscay:
strong of arm and fierce of eye,
he is the lord of the bullring.
He fell for an Andalusian lass,
madly in love fell he;
but the stubborn little miss
answered him this way:
"Five bulls in a single day -
I'll see you kill them all;
and if you win, when you return,
my heart and hand are yours."
"Yes, yes." said he, and off he went,
to the bullring straight away;
five bulls our conquering hero met,
and killed them all that day.

THE OTHERS
Bravo, bravo, this matador -
he showed himself such a champion,
and, in so doing,
he proved his love!

GASTONE AND MATADORS
Then, amidst the applause,
he went back to his love,
and there received the longed-for prize,
wrapped in his sweetheart's arms.

THE OTHERS
It is with tests like this that matadors
sweep lovely women off their feet!

GASTONE AND MATADORS
But here the thing is simpler;
it's enough for us if we can frolic.

TUTTI	**ALL**
Sì, allegri. Or pria tentiamo	Yes, with carefree gaiety. Now first
della sorte il vario umor;	let's try the humour of Fortune;
la palestra dischiudiamo	we'll open the ring
agli audaci giuocator.	to the dauntless gamblers.

(The men unmask. Some of them walk about, talking together, while the others prepare to play. Alfredo enters.)

disc no. 2/track 4 *No, non udrai rimproveri* begins as a stately cabaletta as Germont continues to persuade his son to abandon his love nest. Tension builds (01:54) as he is interrupted by Alfredo, who hasn't heard a word. The scene crashes to a dramatic close (03:24) as Alfredo storms from the house, seeking revenge for his lost love.

TUTTI	**ALL**
Alfredo! Voi!	Alfredo! You!

ALFREDO	**ALFREDO**
Sì, amici -	Yes my friends -

FLORA	**FLORA**
Violetta?	Violetta?

ALFREDO	**ALFREDO**
Non ne so.	I don't know where she is.

TUTTI	**ALL**
Ben disinvolto! Bravo!	How nonchalant! Bravo!
Or via, giuocar si può.	Come, now we can play.

(Gastone cuts the cards. Alfredo and others place their bets. Violetta enters, escorted by the Baron. Flora goes forward to meet her.)

FLORA	**FLORA**
Qui desiata giungi.	I am so glad you have come.

VIOLETTA
Cessi al cortese invito.

FLORA
Grata vi son, barone, d'averlo pur gradito.

BARONE
Germont è qui! Il vedete?

VIOLETTA
Cielo! Gli è vero. Il vedo.

BARONE
Da voi non un sol detto
si volga a questo Alfredo -
non un detto, non un detto!

VIOLETTA
(Ah, perché venni, incauta!
Pietà, gran Dio, di me!)

FLORA (fa sedere Violetta presso di sé sul divano)
Meco t'assidi; narrami -
quai novità vegg'io?

VIOLETTA
I couldn't refuse your kind invitation.

FLORA
I am grateful to you, too, Baron, for
coming.

BARON
Germont is here! Do you see him!

VIOLETTA
Heaven! It's true. I see him.

BARON
You will not say
one word to this Alfredo -
not one word, not one word!

VIOLETTA
(Ah, why was I so rash as to come!
Mercy, oh God!)

FLORA (to Violetta, as she invites her to sit next
to her on thesofa)
Sit here with me, tell me - what is this I
see?

(Dr. Grenvil approaches the two women, who are talking together in a low voice.
The Marquis remains to one side with the Baron. Gastone deals the cards while
Alfredo and various others bet. Still other guests are talking slowly here and there
about the room.)

ALFREDO
Un quattro!

GASTONE
Ancora hai vinto!

ALFREDO
A four!

GASTONE
You win again!

ALFREDO
Sfortuna nell'amore fortuna reca al giuoco.

ALFREDO
Unlucky in love means luck at cards.

(He places his bet and wins again.)

TUTTI
È sempre vincitore!

ALL
He wins every time!

ALFREDO
Oh, vincerò stasera:
e l'oro guadagnato
poscia a goder
tra' campi ritornerò beato.

ALFREDO
Oh, tonight I shall win.
And with the gold
I shall return happily
to the country.

FLORA
Solo?

FLORA
Alone?

ALFREDO
No, no, con tale che vi fu meco ancora,
poi mi sfuggia -

ALFREDO
No, no, with one who was with me,
but ran away -

VIOLETTA
Mio Dio!

VIOLETTA
Oh, God!

GASTONE

GASTONE

(to Alfredo, indicating Violetta)

Pietà di lei!

Take pity on her!

BARONE

BARON

(to Alfredo, making a bad job of restraining his anger)

Signor!

Sir!

VIOLETTA (al Barone)
Frenatevi, o vi lascio.

ALFREDO
Barone, m'appellaste?

BARONE
Siete in sì gran fortuna,
che al giuoco mi tentaste.

ALFREDO (ironico)
Sì? La disfida accetto.

VIOLETTA
Che fia? Morir mi sento!
Pietà, gran Dio, di me!

BARONE (punta)
Cento luigi a destra.

ALFREDO (punta)
Ed alla manca cento.

GASTONE
Un asso - un fante - hai vinto!

BARONE
Il doppio?

ALFREDO
Il doppio sia.

GASTONE (tagliando)
Un quattro, un sette.

VIOLETTA (to the Baron)
Restrain yourself, or I shall leave you.

ALFREDO
Baron, you called me?

BARON
Your luck is so good
I'm tempted to play.

ALFREDO (ironically)
Yes? I accept your challenge.

VIOLETTA
What will happen? I shall die!
Take pity, dear God, take pity on me!

BARON (betting)
A hundred louis on the right.

ALFREDO (betting)
On the left - a hundred.

GASTONE
Ace - jack - you win!

BARON
Double?

ALFREDO
Good - double.

GASTONE (dealing)
Four - seven.

TUTTI
Ancora!

ALFREDO
Pur la vittoria è mia!

CORO
Bravo davver!
La sorte è tutta per Alfredo!

FLORA
Del villeggiar la spesa
farà il baron, già il vedo.

ALFREDO
Seguite pur.

SERVO
La cena è pronta.

FLORA
Andiamo.

CORO *(Tutti partono.)*
Andiamo.

VIOLETTA
(Che fia? morir mi sento!
Pietà, gran Dio, di me!)

ALFREDO *(al Barone)*
Se continuar v'aggrada -

BARONE
Per ora nol possiamo:
più tardi la rivincita.

ALL
Again!

ALFREDO
The victory is mine after all!

CHORUS
Bravo! Really,
luck is on Alfredo's side!

FLORA
The Baron has paid
for the holiday, I see.

ALFREDO
Continue if you wish.

A SERVANT
Dinner is served.

FLORA
Let us go.

CHORUS *(moving towards the table)*
Let us go.

VIOLETTA
(What will happen? I shall die? Take pity,
dear God, take pity on me!)

ALFREDO *(aside, to the Baron)*
If you wish to continue -

BARON
We cannot, for the moment;
we'll play again, later.

ALFREDO
Al giuoco che vorrete.

BARONE
Seguiam gli amici; poscia -

ALFREDO
Sarò qual bramerete - Andiam.

BARONE
Andiam.

ALFREDO
At any game you like.

BARON
Let us follow our friends; later -

ALFREDO
As you wish - let's go.

BARON
Let's go.

(All go out through the centre door; for a moment the scene is deserted. Then Violetta returns, distressed.)

disc no. 2/track 5   In contrast to the drama of the previous scene, Verdi first treats us to the same type of party music we heard at the beginning of the opera.

VIOLETTA
Invitato a qui seguirmi,
verrà desso? Vorrà udirmi?
Ei verrà, ché l'odio atroce
puote in lui più di mia voce.

ALFREDO
Mi chiamaste? Che bramate?

VIOLETTA
Questi luoghi abbandonate,
un periglio vi sovrasta -

ALFREDO
Ah, comprendo! Basta, basta.
E sì vile mi credete?

VIOLETTA
I invited him to follow me.
Will he come? Will he listen to me?
He will come, for his bitter hatred
will bring him, if not my voice.

ALFREDO
You called me? What do you want?

VIOLETTA
Please leave here at once. You are in danger

ALFREDO
Ah, I understand! Enough -
do you think I am such a coward?

VIOLETTA
Ah no, no mai -

ALFREDO
Ma che temete?

VIOLETTA
Tremo sempre del barone.

ALFREDO
È fra noi mortal quistione -
s'ei cadrà per mano mia
un sol colpo vi torria
coll'amante il protettore.
V'atterrisce tal sciagura?

VIOLETTA
Ma s'ei fosse l'uccisore?
Ecco l'unica sventura -
ch'io pavento a me fatale!

ALFREDO
La mia morte! Che ven cale?

VIOLETTA
Deh, partite, e sull'istante.

ALFREDO
Partirò, ma giura innante
che dovunque seguirai
i passi miei.

VIOLETTA
Ah, no, giammai.

ALFREDO
No! giammai?

VIOLETTA
Ah, no, no, never -

ALFREDO
What are you afraid of?

VIOLETTA
I am afraid of the Baron.

ALFREDO
There is bad blood between us -
if he falls into my hands,
a single blow will take away
your lover and your protector.
Would such a misfortune frighten you?

VIOLETTA
But if he should kill you?
That is the only misfortune
which I fear - for it would kill me too!

ALFREDO
My death! What do you care?

VIOLETTA
Ah, leave, leave this minute!

ALFREDO
I shall leave, but first swear
that you will follow me
wherever I go.

VIOLETTA
Ah, no, never.

ALFREDO
No! Never?

VIOLETTA
Va', sciagurato
scorda un nome ch'è infamato.
Va' - mi lascia sul momento -
di fuggirti un giuramento sacro io feci.

ALFREDO
A chi? dillo - chi potea?

VIOLETTA
A chi dritto pien n'avea.

ALFREDO
Fu Douphol?

VIOLETTA
Sì.

ALFREDO
Dunque l'ami?

VIOLETTA
Ebben - l'amo -

ALFREDO

(In a blind fury he runs to the door and calls out.)

Or tutti a me.

(All the guests, bewildered, return to the salon.)

TUTTI
Ne appellaste? Che volete?

VIOLETTA
Go wretched man!
Forget a name which is dishonoured.
Go - leave me this instant -
I took a sacred oath to leave you.

ALFREDO
But who - who could ask it of you?

VIOLETTA
Someone who had full right.

ALFREDO
Was it Douphol?

VIOLETTA
Yes.

ALFREDO
You love him, then?

VIOLETTA
Well - I love him, yes.

ALFREDO

Everyone - come here!

ALL
You called us? What do you want?

ALFREDO

ALFREDO

(pointing to Violetta, who is leaning against the table in utter humiliation)

Questa donna conoscete?

You know this woman?

TUTTI
Chi? Violetta?

ALL
Who? Violetta?

ALFREDO
Che facesse non sapete?

ALFREDO
You don't know what she has done?

VIOLETTA
Ah, taci.

VIOLETTA
Ah, be silent.

TUTTI
No.

ALL
No.

disc no. 2
track 6&7

Verdi interrupts the action with these Gypsy and Spanish entertainments. This lively music gives us a rest from the tension in the plot. These foreign melodies also give the opera broader appeal, and the dance-like elements made adapting the work for the Paris Opera easier. At the time, the Paris Opera required ballet sequences in all operatic works performed there.

ALFREDO
Ogni suo aver tal femmina
per amor mio sperdea.
Io cieco, vile, misero,
tutto accettar potea.
Ma è tempo ancora! Tergermi
da tanta macchia bramo.
Qui testimon vi chiamo
che qui pagato io l'ho.

ALFREDO
This woman was about to lose
all she owns for love of me;
while I, blinded, vile, wretched,
was capable of accepting everything.
But there is still time! I wish
to cleanse myself of such a stain.
I have called you here as witnesses
that I have paid her all I owe.

(With furious contempt, he throws a purse down at Violetta's feet. Violetta faints in the arms of Flora. As Alfredo is speaking the last few words, his father enters.)

TUTTI
Oh, infamia orribile tu commettesti!
Un cor sensibile così uccidesti!
Di donne ignobile insultatore,
di qui allontanati, ne desti orror!
Va', va', ne desti orror!
Di donne ignobile insultator, ecc.

ALL
Oh, what a terrible thing you have done!
You have killed a sensitive heart!
Ignoble man, to insult a woman so,
leave this house at once, you fill us with
horror! Go, go, you fill us with horror!
Ignoble man, to insult a woman, etc.

GERMONT
Di sprezzo degno sé stesso rende
chi pur nell'ira la donna offende.
Dov'è mio figlio? Più non lo vedo:
in te più Alfredo trovar non so.

GERMONT
Whoever, even in anger, offends a woman
exposes himself to the contempt of all.
Where is my son? I cannot find him,
for in you I no longer see Alfredo.

ALFREDO
Ah, sì - che feci! Ne sento orrore.
Gelosa smania, deluso amore
mi strazian l'alma; più non ragiono.
Da lei perdono più non avrò.
Volea fuggirla - non ho potuto!
Dall'ira spinto son qui venuto!
Or che lo sdegno ho disfogato,
me sciagurato! rimorso n'ho.

ALFREDO
Ah, yes - what have I done? I am horrified.
Maddening jealousy, disillusioned love
torture my heart - I have lost my reason.
She can never forgive me now,
I tried to flee from her - I couldn't!
I came here, spurred on by anger!
Now that I have vented my fury,
I am sick with remorse - oh, wretched man!

TUTTI *(a Violetta)*
Oh, quanto peni! Ma pur fa cor.
Qui soffre ognuno del tuo dolor;
fra cari amici qui sei soltanto;
rasciuga il pianto che t'inondò.

ALL *(to Violetta)*
Ah, how you suffer! But take heart,
here, each of us suffers for your sorrow;
you are here among dear friends;
dry the tears which bathe your face.

GERMONT *(da sé)*
Io sol fra tanti so qual virtude
di quella misera il sen racchiude.

GERMONT *(to himself)*
I alone among these people know
what virtue there is in this poor woman's

Io so che l'ama, che gli è fedele,
eppur crudele tacer dovrò!

BARONE (piano, ad Alfredo)
A questa donna l'atroce insulto
qui tutti offese, ma non inulto
fia tanto oltraggio - provar vi voglio
che il vostro orgoglio fiaccar saprò.

ALFREDO (da sé)
Ohimé, che feci! Ne sento orrore, ecc.
Da lei perdono più non avrò.

heart. I know she loves him, is faithful to
him, and yet I must keep a pitiless silence!

BARON (in a low voice, to Alfredo)
The atrocious insult to this woman
has shocked us all, but such an outrage
shall not go unavenged. I will show you
that I am well able to break your pride.

ALFREDO (to himself)
Alas, what have I done, etc.
I am horrified she can never forgive me
now.

disc no. 2/track 8 Tension resumes as the card game begins (00:33), and the vocal lines take on a
static quality with the exception of Violetta's asides (01:14, 02:26 and 03:20),
which soar out over the texture expressing her distress.

VIOLETTA (riavendosi)
Alfredo, Alfredo, di questo core
non puoi comprendere tutto l'amore;
tu non conosci che fino a prezzo
del tuo disprezzo provato io l'ho!

TUTTI (a Violetta)
Quanto peni! fa cor!

ALFREDO
Ohimè! che feci! Ne sento orror!

VIOLETTA
Ma verrà tempo in che il saprai -
come t'amassi confesserai.
Dio dai rimorsi ti salvi allora, ah!
Io spenta ancora pur t'amerò.

VIOLETTA (regaining consciousness)
Alfredo, Alfredo you cannot understand
fully the love I have in my heart;
you do not know that even at the risk
of your disdain I have put it to the test!

ALL (to Violetta)
How you suffer! But take heart!

ALFREDO
Alas, what have I done? I am horrified!

VIOLETTA
But the day will come when you will know
-You will admit how much I loved you.
May God save you, then, from remorse,
I shall be dead, but I shall love you still.

ALFREDO
Ohimè! che feci! Ne sento orror!

BARONE
Provar vi voglio che tanto
orgoglio fiaccar saprò.

GERMONT
Io so che l'ama, che gli è fedele,
eppur crudele tacer dovrò!

TUTTI
Quanto peni! fa cor! ecc.

ALFREDO
Alas, what have I done? I am horrified!

BARON
I will show you that I am well able
to break your pride.

GERMONT
I know she loves him, is faithful to him,
and yet I must keep a pitiless silence!

ALL
How you suffer! Take heart! etc.

(Germont leads his son away with him; the Baron follows him. Flora and the Doctor accompany Violetta to her room. The others go out.)

Act 3

PRELUDE

Violetta's bedroom. Upstage, a bed with half-drawn curtains; a window with inside shutters; next to the bed a low table with a water-bottle, a glass, various medicines. Downstage, a dressing-table; nearby a sofa; another table with a night-lamp; several chairs and other pieces. The door is to the left; opposite, a fireplace, with a low fire.

(Violetta is in bed, asleep. Annina, sitting in a chair near the fireplace, has dozed off.)

disc no. 2/track 9 Violetta and Alfredo confront one another over a taut musical accompaniment which reflects his insanely jealous bravado.

disc no. 2/track 10 Alfredo curses Violetta in a brief aria over a cabaletta-style figure in the orchestra. The guests respond wildly (00:58), their incredulity underlined by an unresolved closing chord.

VIOLETTA
Annina?

ANNINA
Comandate?

VIOLETTA
Dormivi, poveretta?

ANNINA
Sì, perdonate.

VIOLETTA
Dammi d'acqua un sorso.

VIOLETTA
Annina?

ANNINA
Yes, madam?

VIOLETTA
Were you sleeping, poor child?

ANNINA
Yes. Forgive me.

VIOLETTA
Give me a sip of water.

(Annina does so.)

Osserva, è pieno il giorno?

ANNINA
Son sett'ore.

VIOLETTA
Dà accesso a un po' di luce.

(Annina opens the blinds and looks out into the street.)

ANNINA
Il signor di Grenvil!

VIOLETTA
Oh, il vero amico!
Alzar mi vo' - m'aita.

VIOLETTA
Quanta bontà!
pensaste a me per tempo!

DOTTORE *(Le tocca il polso.)*
Sì, come vi sentite?

VIOLETTA
Soffre il mio corpo.
Ma tranquilla ho l'alma.
Mi confortò ier sera un pio ministro.
Ah, religione è sollievo ai sofferenti.

Look outside and tell me - is it still day?

ANNINA
It's seven o'clock.

VIOLETTA
Open the blinds a little.

ANNINA
Doctor Grenvil!

VIOLETTA
Oh, he's a true friend!
I want to get up. Help me.

(She gets up then falls back on the bed. Finally, supported by Annina, she gets up and walks slowly to the sofa. The doctor enters in time to help her get comfortable. Annina brings cushions and puts them behind her.)

VIOLETTA
How good you are!
you thought of me in time!

DOCTOR *(feeling her pulse)*
Yes. How do you feel?

VIOLETTA
My body suffers, but my soul is in peace.
Last evening a priest came to comfort me.
Religion is a great consolation to the
suffering.

DOTTORE
E questa notte?

VIOLETTA
Ebbi tranquillo il sonno.

DOTTORE
Coraggio adunque - la convalescenza
non è lontana.

VIOLETTA
Oh, la bugia pietosa
ai medici è concessa.

DOTTORE (*Le stringe la mano.*)
Addio - a più tardi.

VIOLETTA
Non mi scordate.

ANNINA

(in a low voice, as she shows the doctor out)

Come va, signore?

DOTTORE
La tisi non le accorda che poche ore.

ANNINA
Or fate cor.

VIOLETTA
Giorno di festa è questo?

DOCTOR
And during the night?

VIOLETTA
I slept quite peacefully.

DOCTOR
Courage, then. Your convalescence is not
far off.

VIOLETTA
Oh, the little white lie
is permissible in a doctor.

DOCTOR (*pressing her hand*)
Goodbye - I'll come back later.

VIOLETTA
Don't forget me.

ANNINA

How is she, sir?

DOCTOR
She has only a few hours to live.

ANNINA
Take heart, now.

VIOLETTA
Today is a holiday?

ANNINA
Tutta Parigi impazza - è carnevale!

VIOLETTA
Ah, nel comun tripudio, sallo Iddio
quanti infelici soffron! Quale somma
v'ha in quello stipo?

(pointing)

ANNINA

(opening the drawer and counting the money)

Venti luigi.

VIOLETTA
Dieci ne reca a' poveri tu stessa.

ANNINA
Poco rimanvi allora -

VIOLETTA
Oh, mi saran bastanti.
Cerca poscia mie lettere.

ANNINA
Ma voi?

VIOLETTA
Nulla occorrà - sollecita, se puoi.

(Annina goes out.)

VIOLETTA

(she takes a letter from her bosom and reads:)

ANNINA
Paris is going mad - it's carnival.

VIOLETTA
Oh, in all this merrymaking, heaven knows
how many poor ones are suffering! How
much is there in that drawer?

ANNINA

Twenty louis.

VIOLETTA
Take ten and give them to the poor.

ANNINA
There won't be much left -

VIOLETTA
Oh, for me it will be enough.
Then bring in my letters.

ANNINA
But you, madam?

VIOLETTA
Nothing will happen - go quickly, please

VIOLETTA

disc no. 2/track 11 As with all of Germont's music, he responds here in expansive fatherly phrases. Alfredo, realizing what he has done, responds in halting phrases (00:50) as he tries to excuse his actions.

disc no. 2/track 12 This large ensemble, in which everyone expresses their various thoughts at once, brings the act to a stunning conclusion. It is a nineteenth-century operatic convention in which the drama is not advanced. The main point here is four minutes and eighteen seconds of beautiful singing.

"Teneste la promessa - la disfida ebbe
luogo! Il Barone fu ferito però migliora.
Alfredo è in stranio suolo; il vostro
sacrifizio io stesso gli ho svelato; egli
a voi tornerà pel suo perdono; io pur verrò.
Curatevi - mertate un avvenir migliore.
Giorgio Germont."
È tardi!
Attendo, attendo - né a me giungon mai!

"You kept your promise. The duel has
taken place! The Baron was wounded, but
is recovering. Alfredo has gone abroad; I
myself revealed your sacrifice to him; he
will return to ask your pardon; I too shall
come. Take care of yourself. You deserve a
happier future. Giorgio Germont".
It is late!
I wait, I wait - they never come to me!

(She looks at herself in the mirror.)

Oh, come son mutata!
Ma il dottore a sperar pure m'esorta!
Ah, con tal morbo ogni speranza è morta.
Addio, del passato bei sogni ridenti,
le rose del volto già sono pallenti;
l'amore d'Alfredo perfino mi manca,
conforto, sostegno dell'anima stanca -
conforto, sostegno -
Ah, della traviata sorridi al desio;
a lei, deh, perdona; tu accoglila, o Dio!
Ah! - Tutto,
tutto finì, or tutto, tutto finì.

Ah, how I have changed!
But the doctor still gives me hope!
Ah, with this disease every hope is dead.
Adieu, sweet, happy dreams of the past,
the roses of my cheeks are already fading.
I miss so much Alfredo's love,
which once solaced my weary soul -
Solaced and comforted -
Ah, smile upon the woman who has
strayed; forgive her, oh God, grant she may
come to thee!
Now all is finished, all is over.

The Prelude begins with the same sorrowful music we heard in the Prelude to act I. This is followed by an extended lament which seems to express the alternating hope and despair of Violetta's situation.

CORO DI MASCHERE	**CHORUS OF MASQUERADERS**
(dall'esterno)	*(from the street)*
Largo al quadrupede sir della festa,	Make way for the quadruped King of the
di fiori e pampini	festival, Wearing his crown of flowers
cinta la testa.	and vine leaves. Make way for the tamest of
Largo al più docil d'ogni cornuto,	all who wear horns, greet him with music
di corni e pifferi abbia il saluto.	of horn and flute. People of Paris,
Parigini, date passo, al trionfo del Bue gras-	open the path to the triumphant Fattened
so. L'Asia né l'Africa	Ox. Neither Asia nor Africa
vide il più bello, vanto ed orgoglio d'ogni	has ever seen better, this pride and joy of
macello. Allegre maschere, pazzi garzoni,	the butcher's trade. Light-hearted maidens,
tutti plauditelo con canti e suoni!	and frolicking lads, pay him due honour
Parigini, date passo,	of music and song! People of Paris, open
al trionfo del Bue grasso.	the path to the triumphant Fattened Ox.
Largo al quadrupede sir della festa,	Make way for the quadruped King of the
di fiori e pampini	festival wearing his crown of flowers
cinta la testa.	and vine leaves.

(Annina returns, hastily.)

ANNINA *(esitando)*	**ANNINA** *(hesitating)*
Signora!	Madam!
VIOLETTA	**VIOLETTA**
Che t'accadde?	What has happened?
ANNINA	**ANNINA**
Quest'oggi, è vero, vi sentite meglio?	Today you feel better, don't you?
VIOLETTA	**VIOLETTA**
Sì, perché?	Yes, why?

ANNINA
D'esser calma promettete?

VIOLETTA
Sì, che vuoi dirmi?

ANNINA
Prevenir vi volli -
un gioia improvvisa!

VIOLETTA
Una gioia! Dicesti?

ANNINA
Sì, o signora -

VIOLETTA
Alfredo! Ah, tu il vedesti?
Ei vien! T'affretta.

(Annina nods her head, then goes to open the door.)

Alfredo!

(Alfredo enters, pale with emotion. They are in each other's arms as they exclaim:)

Amato Alfredo! Oh gioia!

ALFREDO
Oh mia Violetta. Oh gioia!
Colpevol sono - so tutto,
 o cara.

ANNINA
Do you promise not to get excited?

VIOLETTA
Yes. What do you want to tell me?

ANNINA
I wanted to prepare you -
A happy surprise!

VIOLETTA
Did you say - a surprise?

ANNINA
Oh yes, madam -

VIOLETTA
Alfredo! Ah, you saw him?
He is coming! Oh, quickly!

Alfredo!

Beloved Alfredo! Oh joy!

ALFREDO
My Violetta! Oh, joy!
The fault is mine - I know everything now,
dear.

VIOLETTA
Io so che alfine reso mi sei!

ALFREDO
Da questo palpito s'io t'ami impara,
senza te esistere più non potrei.

VIOLETTA
Ah, s'anco in vita m'hai ritrovata,
credi che uccidere non può il dolor.

ALFREDO
Scorda l'affanno, donna adorata,
a me perdona e al genitor.

VIOLETTA
Ch'io ti perdoni? La rea son io;
ma solo amor tal mi rendé.

ALFREDO, VIOLETTA
Null'uomo o demon, angel mio,
mai più dividermi potrà da te.

VIOLETTA
I know only that you have come back!

ALFREDO
Let my emotion teach you how I love you.
I cannot live without you.

VIOLETTA
Ah, if you have found me still alive,
it means grief has not the power to kill.

ALFREDO
Forget your sorrow, my adored one,
and forgive my father and me.

VIOLETTA
What is there to forgive? The guilty one is
me; but it was love alone which made me
so.

ALFREDO, VIOLETTA
Now neither man nor demon, my angel,
will ever be able to take you away.

disc no. 2/track 15 As Violetta reads Germont's letter, we hear a solo violin echo the theme to which
Alfredo first poured out his love in act I.

ALFREDO
Parigi, o cara, noi lasceremo,
la vita uniti trascorreremo;
de' corsi affanni compenso avrai,
la tua salute rifiorirà.
Sospiro e luce tu mi sarai,
tutto il futuro ne arriderà.

ALFREDO
From Paris dear, we shall go away,
to live our lives together.
We shall make up for all our heartache,
your health will come back again.
You will be the light of my life,
the future will smile upon us.

VIOLETTA

(echoing him as in a dream)

Parigi, o caro, noi lasceremo,
la vita uniti trascorreremo:

ALFREDO
Sì.
De' corsi affanni compenso avrai.
La tua salute rifiorirà.
Sospiro e luce tu mi sarai, ecc.

VIOLETTA

From Paris dear, we shall go away,
to live our loves together...

ALFREDO
Yes.
We shall make up for all our heartache.
Your health will come back again.
You will be the light of my life, etc.

disc no. 2/track 16 *Addio del passato*. This famous aria is a masterpiece of construction. Introduced by a melancholy solo oboe, Violetta's farewells are accompanied by halting figures in the orchestra that call to mind her shortness of breath. As she recalls Alfredo's love (00:58) her lines begin to soar, and as she prays for redemption the orchestra presses forward in an ascending harmonic progression (02:05). Having expended all her energies, her line descends, punctuated by isolated chords in the strings, and she ends on an unaccompanied high A (03:26).

VIOLETTA
Ah, non più, a un tempio -
Alfredo, andiamo,
del tuo ritorno grazie rendiamo.

(She sways, as if to fall.)

ALFREDO
Tu impallidisci -

VIOLETTA
È nulla, sai!
Gioia improvvisa non entra mai,
senza turbarlo, in mesto core.

VIOLETTA
No more now, Alfredo let us go to church
to offer thanks
for your return.

ALFREDO
You are pale -

VIOLETTA
It is nothing!
Such sudden joy cannot come
to a sorrowing heart without disturbing it.

(She throws herself down, upon a chair; her head falls back.)

ALFREDO *(spaventato, sorreggendola)*
Gran Dio! Violetta!

ALFREDO *(holding her up, terrified)*
Great God! Violetta!

VIOLETTA *(sforzandosi)*
È il mio malore -
fu debolezza! Ora son forte.
Vedi? Sorrido.

VIOLETTA *(with great effort)*
It's my illness -
A moment of weakness! Now I am strong.
See? I am smiling.

ALFREDO
Ahi, cruda sorte!

ALFREDO
Ah, cruel destiny!

VIOLETTA
Fu nulla. Annina, dammi a vestire.

VIOLETTA
It was nothing. Annina, bring me my dress.

ALFREDO
Adesso? Attendi.

ALFREDO
Now? Wait.

VIOLETTA
No - voglio uscire.

VIOLETTA
No. I want to go out.

(Annina gives her a dress which she tries to put on.
Too weak to succeed, she exclaims:)

Gran Dio! Non posso!

Dear God! I cannot!

ALFREDO
(Cielo! Che vedo!)

ALFREDO
(Heaven! What is this!)

(to Annina)

Va' pel dottore.

Go to call the doctor.

disc no. 2/track 17 The revelers outside underline the marked contrast between Violetta's former life and the darkened room in which she now awaits her death.

VIOLETTA

Ah! Digli che Alfredo
è ritornato all'amor mio -
Digli che vivere ancor vogl'io.

VIOLETTA

Tell him that Alfredo
has come back to his love.
Tell him I want to live again.

(Annina goes out. Then, to Alfredo:)

Ma se tornando non m'hai salvato,
a niuno in terra salvarmi è dato.
Ah! gran Dio! Morir sì giovine,
io che penato ho tanto!
Morir sì presso a tergere
il mio sì lungo pianto!
Ah, dunque fu delirio
la credula speranza;
invano di costanza
armato avrò il mio cor!

If in returning you have not saved my life,
then nothing on earth can save me.
Ah! Dear God! To die so young.
when I have sorrowed so long!
To die, when now, at last,
I might have ceased my weeping!
Ah, it was but a dream,
my credulous hope;
to sheathe my heart in constancy
was all in vain.

ALFREDO

Oh mio sospiro e palpito,
diletto del cor mio!
Le mie colle tue lagrime
confondere degg'io -
Ma più che mai, deh credilo,
m'è d'uopo di costanza.
Ah, tutto alla speranza
non chiudere il tuo cor.
Ah! Violetta mia, deh calmati,
m'uccide il tuo dolor deh, calmati!

ALFREDO

My very breath of life, sweet
pulse of my heart!
My tears must flow
together with yours.
But more than ever, ah, believe me,
we have need of constancy.
Ah! Do not close
your heart to hope.
Ah, my Violetta, be calm,
you grief is killing me, be calm!

VIOLETTA

Oh Alfredo! il crudo termine
serbato al nostro amor!

VIOLETTA

Oh, Alfredo, what a cruel end
for our love!

(Violetta sinks down upon the sofa. Germont enters, followed after a moment by Dr. Grenvil.)

The excitement moves inside as Annina enters. The harmonies remain unstable—
their direction uncertain—until we hear the news of Alfredo's imminent return,
and all resolves in an optimistic major key.

GERMONT
Ah, Violetta!

VIOLETTA
Voi, signor!

ALFREDO
Mio padre!

VIOLETTA
Non mi scordaste?

GERMONT
La promessa adempio.
A stringervi qual figlia vengo al seno,
o generosa!

VIOLETTA
Ahimè, tardi giungeste!

(She embraces him.)

Pure, grata ven sono.
Grenvil, vedete? Fra le braccia io spiro
di quanti cari ho al mondo.

GERMONT
Che mai dite!
(Oh cielo - è ver!)

ALFREDO
La vedi, padre mio?

GERMONT
Ah, Violetta!

VIOLETTA
You, sir!

ALFREDO
Father!

VIOLETTA
You had not forgotten me?

GERMONT
I am fulfilling my promise.
I have come to embrace you as a daughter.
O generous woman!

VIOLETTA
Alas, you have come too late!

But I am grateful to you.
Grenvil, see? I am dying in the arms
of the only dear ones I have.

GERMONT
What are you saying!
(Oh, heaven, it is true!)

ALFREDO
Do you see her, father?

GERMONT

Di più non lacerarmi.
Troppo rimorso l'alma mi divora.
Quasi fulmin m'atterra ogni suo detto.
Oh, malcauto vegliardo!
Il mal ch'io feci ora sol vedo!

VIOLETTA

GERMONT

Don't torture me any longer.
My soul is already devoured by remorse.
Every word she speaks is a thunderbolt.
Oh, rash old man!
Only now do I see the harm I have done.

VIOLETTA

(Meanwhile, with great difficulty, she has opened a secret drawer of her dressing table. She takes from it a medallion and gives it to Alfredo.)

disc no. 2/ track 19 *Parigi, o cara.* This famous duet, in which the lovers describe an idyllic future together, is often performed in concert.

Più a me t'appressa -
Ascolta, amato Alfredo.
Prendi, quest'è l'immagine de' miei passati
giorni; a rammentarti torni
colei che sì t'amò.

Come nearer to me -
Listen, beloved Alfredo.
Take this, it is a portrait painted some years
ago. It will help you to remember
the one who loved you so.

ALFREDO

No, non morrai, non dirmelo -
Dei viver, amor mio.
A strazio sì terribil
qui non mi trasse Iddio.

ALFREDO

Ah, you will not die, don't tell me so -
You must live, my darling.
God did not bring me back to you
to face such a tragedy.

GERMONT

Cara, sublime, sublime vittima
d'un disperato amore,
perdonami lo strazio recato al tuo bel cor.

GERMONT

Dear noble victim of a hopeless love,
forgive me for having made your heart
suffer.

We hear Violetta's heart beat faster as she tries to take up her life again, but the
low strings repeatedly interject short descending phrases which punctuate her
failures.

VIOLETTA
Se una pudica vergine degli anni suoi sul
fiore, a te donasse il core -
sposa ti sia - lo vo'.
Le porgi quest'effigie;
dille che dono ell'è di chi nel ciel tra gli
angeli prega per lei, per te.

VIOLETTA
If some young girl in the flower of life
should give her heart to you - marry her - I
wish it. Then give her this portrait:
Tell her it is the gift of one who, in heaven
among the angels, prays for her and for you.

GERMONT
Finché avrà il ciglio lagrime
io piangerò per te.
Vola a' beati spiriti,
Iddio ti chiama a sé.

GERMONT
As long as my eyes have tears,
so long shall I weep for you.
Fly to the realm of the blessed,
God calls you unto him.

ALFREDO
Sì presto, ah no, dividerti
morte non può da me.
Ah, vivi, o solo un feretro
m'accoglierà con te.

ALFREDO
So soon, oh no, death
cannot take you from me.
Ah, live, or a single coffin
will receive me as well as you.

VIOLETTA *(rianimata)*
È strano!
Cessarono gli spasimi del dolore.
In me rinasce - m'agita insolito vigor!
Ah! ma io ritorno a viver!
Oh gioia!

VIOLETTA *(getting up, as if reinvigorated)*
How strange!
The spasms of pain have ceased:
A strange vigour has brought me to life!
Ah! I shall live -
Oh, joy!

(She falls down, senseless, upon the sofa.)

Finally resigned to her fate, Violetta gives her medallion to Alfredo over a funeral march motive in the orchestra which becomes more insistent as Alfredo and his father pour out their despair. As Violetta slips away, the key becomes major (01:07), but it is still punctuated by the funereal figure—we hear both heaven and earth. Over shimmering strings, a solo violin once again announces the love theme (03:22). It grows in intensity as she rallies one last time, and at the peak of her ecstasy, she falls dead and the orchestra hurdles toward its final tragic D-flat minor chord.

FINE   END

La Traviata

GIACOMO PUCCINI

COMPACT DISC ONE   67:32:00

1	Prelude	4:31

Atto Primo/Act One

2	Dell'invito tracorsa è gia l'ora	5:02
3	LIbiamo ne'lieti calici	3:02
	Alfredo/Violetta	
4	Che è ciò?	2:24
5	Un dì, felice eterea	3:33
	Alfredo/Violetta	
6	Ebben? Che diavol fate?	1:27
7	Si ridesta in ciel l'aurora	1:53
	tutti	
8	È strano	1:28
	Violetta	
9	Ah, fors'è lui	5:59
	Violetta	
10	Follie! Follie!	1:15
	Violetta	
11	Sempre libera	3:49
	Violetta	

COMPACT DISC TWO   70:26:00